PL 4/ p 86

اور سر او اعلان

Mate in Two Moves

THE TWO-MOVE CHESS PROBLEM MADE EASY

BRIAN HARLEY
Chess Editor of The Observer

DOVER PUBLICATIONS, INC.
NEW YORK

DEDICATED TO MY WIFE

Published in Canada by General Publishing Company, Ltd., 30 Lesmill Road, Don Mills, Toronto, Ontario.

Published in the United Kingdom by Constable and Company, Ltd., 10 Orange Street, London WC 2.

This Dover edition, first published in 1970, is an unabridged and unaltered republication of the work originally published in 1931. It is reprinted by special arrangement with the original publisher, G. Bell & Sons, Ltd., London.

Standard Book Number: 486-22434-1
Library of Congress Catalog Card Number: 70-100542

Manufactured in the United States of America
Dover Publications, Inc.
180 Varick Street
New York, N.Y. 10014

CONTENTS

CHAPTER I

INTRODUCTION

A chess problem may be defined as a position constructed to display, to best advantage, an idea (or combination of ideas) that leads to forced mate in a definite number of moves. The composer of a problem may wish to illustrate a series of ingenious attacking or defending manoeuvres, or he may concentrate on other points, such as pure deception of the solver, a peculiar set of mating positions, repetition of a particular strategic device, or just a whimsical fancy of his own. In any case, he has a fundamental advantage over the game player from the artist's point of view—he does what he likes with both the White and Black men, and makes them equally subservient to his will.

In problems a great deal of the essence of chess is packed into a few moves, instead of being sandwiched into the desert waste of routine and inexact tactics that occur in even the best-played games. There are, of course, several facets of chess that do not shine in the problem, such as "playing for position," pawn and other endings, but in brilliant and critical strokes it easily surpasses the possibilities of actual play.

Problems appeal more to the artist within us than to the fighting spirit, for here we are not so much concerned with the fact that one of the players (White, by convention) is certainly going to win, as with the manner in which he achieves his aim. Chessplayers are often heard to criticise problem positions on the grounds that "Black is not given a chance," coolly disregarding the time-limit imposed upon White. In many a problem, a subtle defence is as prominent as the attack, and White may have almost as much difficulty in carrying out the contract as his opponent has, in his efforts to defeat it. It is beside the point to say that White has an overwhelming force (not always the case, however) and could *win* anyhow he liked. The real point is that he has only one way, and not an obvious way, of mating in X moves. To repeat an old simile, in playing or watching a game of chess, you are in the presence of a real fight, generally conducted in somewhat brutal fashion—kicking, biting, and gouging are all within the rules; in a problem you look on at an exhibition bout, carefully pre-arranged to display the best qualities of both opponents.

Throughout this book the English notation has been adopted; it is rather cumbrous, but much more familiar to the average British or American chess enthusiast than the Algebraic method. For the benefit of the novice, a full explanation is given by means of the following diagram. A knowledge of the movements of the different pieces is assumed, but nothing else.

Files: QR QKt QB Q K KB KKt KR
(uprights)

First of all, the pieces are denominated by the capital that begins their names, K for King 🨄 🨔 ; Q for Queen 🨁 🨑 ; R for Rook (or Castle) 🨂 🨒 ; B for Bishop 🨃 🨓 ; P for Pawn 🨅 🨕 ; with Kt distinguishing the Knight 🨄 🨔. The White forces are invariably assumed to play from the lower half of the board, and to have the first move.

Names of the squares.—These follow the perpendicular lines on the board, called *files*, the horizontal lines being the *ranks*. In the diagram, the White Rooks are on the same file, and the Black Rooks on the same rank. The files are named by the pieces placed on them at the beginning of the game, that on the extreme left being called the Queen's Rook's or Q R file, and so on, as shown in the diagram. The *numbers* of the squares follow the distance from the original piece of the *same colour* as the moving piece, each square having two possible numbers. For example, if White should play his R into the extreme left hand corner, it would be described as R – R 1 (Rook to Rook's *one*) but if the Black Kt should go to the same square, we should have Kt – R 8 (Knight to Rook's *eight*).

A convention of problem notation is illustrated by the White Knights in the diagram. Either, it will be seen, can play to Kt 6, and, if this square is chosen, we discriminate the Knights by the files from which they start, that nearer the right hand side of the board being called the K Kt (on R 4 in the diagram) and the other the Q Kt. Q Kt – Kt 6 accordingly refers to the move, Kt on B 4 – Kt 6. So with the Black Rooks: K R – Kt 2 refers to the R on B 2. This little economy of notation will not help with the White move R – B 2, since both pieces are on the same file, and we must here discriminate by saying R (B 1), or R (B 3), – B 2. In dealing with the Pawns, however, this method is not employed, as they are named definitely from the files on which they stand in the position. Q P means the P on Q file, and *not* a P nearer the left hand side than another. Thus we have (White) P – Q Kt 4 (Black in reply) R P × P (capture is denoted by the ×) or B P × P, as he chooses. Black may also capture this White P by the P on his R 5 *en passant*, described as P×P *e.p.* when his P remains on Q Kt 6. Notice that it is necessary to say P – Q Kt 4 for White and not simply P – Kt 4, since his K Kt P can also move forward two squares, but that in the Black reply it is not necessary to use a prefix.

Early problems were, naturally enough, simple affairs and rather puzzles than what we should now consider legitimate positions. Special conditions were often made, that mate must be given with a particular piece, that a certain unit could not be captured, and so on. In mediaeval times a good deal of money was lost and won in bets on these freakish positions. Below is given a thirteenth century composition from a famous Florentine collection, called the "Bonus Socius," from which the late "Good Companion Chess Club," a great international organisation with its head-quarters in the U.S.A., derived its name.

No. 1 ANTIQUE PROBLEM

Author unknown.   Good Companion M.S. (Miniature)

Mate in 2

(This means that White moves first and must force mate on his second move against any defence.)

Solution:—1. K R (K R 7) – K Kt 7, and whatever Black replies, one of the R's will go to the eighth rank, delivering mate. This is quite a pretty bit of strategy, though much too elementary for modern taste. A *Miniature* is the sub-title given to any problem of seven units or less, while those of eight to twelve are called *Merediths*, after an American composer, who favoured light positions (see No. 2). White's first move is called the *Key move*, or *Key*.

Very little development took place in problems for some hundreds of years. In fact, it was not until the nineteenth century that composers attained full art-consciousness. Previous to this era, many great players arose, founded schools of chess, particularly in Italy, Spain and France, studied and constructed end-games, and published books full of their theories and analyses, but the limitation of the number of moves in which mate must be given—the fundamental difference between a problem and a game of chess—does not seem to have interested them very much. Even when, about 100 years ago, problems began to be produced in large numbers, their composers showed themselves to be obsessed, to a great extent, by conventions based purely on the game. Play continued for an inordinate number of moves, and the defence was very restricted. Sacrifice of force by the attack, a stratagem belonging more essentially to the game than to the problem art, was almost the only idea, and it was generally conducted by a series of checks, the Black K picking up a hatful of White pieces on the way to his doom. Not much subtlety was shown in compelling the solution, White's own K often being exposed, and threatened with immediate disaster unless something drastic was done. In order to make the problem position appear as much like a game ending as possible, the composer added a number of pieces, which had no use whatever in the solution, but more or less equalised the forces. This process, known as "dressing the board," is at complete variance with the modern theory of economy of force. No. 2 is an example of the "game-players" problem; a favourable example, for the solution is not unduly long and there is not much "board-dressing."

No. 2 OLD TYPE PROBLEM (MEREDITH)

S. Loyd.   Leslie's Illustrated Newspaper, 1856

Mate in 4

1. R × Kt ch (Key move). K × R (if R × R, 2. Q – K2 mate).
2. R – Q2 ch K × R (if K else, 3. Q – K1 mate).
3. Q – K1 ch and mates next move.

An orgy of sacrifice, a classic of its type.   Notice that the White K stands to be shot at by practically the whole Black force, an indication of a checking solution throughout.

Modern aesthetic standards can be briefly summed up as follows :

(1) There should be no unit on the board that is not absolutely necessary to the composer's idea, or "theme," as we may call it.   (2) The Black defence should be given as wide a latitude as possible of alternatives that compel quite different attacks by White, and extend him to the full length of his contract—a feature sadly lacking in Problem No. 2.

6

It follows from standard (2) that violent key moves, such as checks, captures and other restrictions of the Black forces, are, generally speaking, inferior, while standard (1) besides complying with an ideal of all art, strict economy of means in carrying out an idea, renders possible many complex themes, that could not be presented at all, if any material were wasted.

Besides these aesthetic canons, a few rules have become standardised. They are as follows :—

(1) A problem must be a *possible* position in a game of chess; (it need not be, in fact it rarely is, a *probable* one) with one exception. The use in the diagram of two Q's, or three R's, B's or Kt's, of the same colour, is forbidden by a rigid convention, but such duplication of force may, and often does occur by pawn promotion in the course of the play. Very likely a future generation will see some modification of this convention, when combinations under present conditions show signs of exhaustion.

(2) A good many problemists object also to a piece in the diagram that *must* have been due to pawn promotion in the hypothetical game that precedes the position; for example a KB on (say) KR3, with the KP and K Kt P in the diagram on their original squares. Obviously such "obtrusive force," as it is called, can be due only to P=B (Pawn promotes to Bishop) at some stage of the game. The general opinion, as voiced by a recent meeting of the British Chess Problem Society, is that "obtrusive force" is permissible, but counts as a demerit. Personally, I have very little objection to such force. As it is not absolutely forbidden, it can be criticised only on the grounds of improbability of play in the game, and much more unlikely manoeuvres than peculiar P promotions must have occurred in the antecedents of many problems. Some ultra-purists may object to a definite P promotion in the game, even if the offending unit has been removed before the problem position occurred. Its antecedents are not *quite* respectable.

(3) *As a key move*, P × P *en passant* is allowed, only if it

7

can be absolutely proved that Black's last move, made in the assumed game just before the problem position arose, was the double leap of the P that is to be captured. *After the Key move*, it can of course occur, subject to the usual rules of the game. Here is an example of the manoeuvre as a Key:

No. 3 P × P *EN PASSANT* KEY

F. Amelung. *Düna Zeitung*, 1897

Mate in 2

To solve this problem, one must examine the move just made by Black that gave rise to the diagram position. Take the K first; Kt2 is the only plausible square from which he might have departed. This is ruled out, when one realises that he would have been in check from a White P that could not have reached B6 on *WHITE'S* last move. Therefore the Black KtP must have been the unit that moved last. It could not have come from B3 or R3, capturing White force, as these squares are occupied. Nor could it have played from Kt3, for then the White K would have been in check, *with Black to move*. By elimination, therefore, Black's last move must have been P from Kt2 to Kt4, and White can

legally play as his Key move 1. P × P *e.p.* Black must reply
K – R4, when 2. R × P is mate. The above process of
proving how a problem position must have arisen is called
Retrograde Analysis, and it is the subject of a book by T. R.
Dawson and W. Hundsdorfer, edited by A. C. White. The
last-named is the Patron-Saint of Problemdom, and has published and edited (sometimes in collaboration) no less than
thirty-seven books on the art. He is an American, who has
sat at the feet of Sam Loyd in his youth, and has built up
an all-inclusive collection of problems, now in the hands of
George Hume, of Nottingham. Problemists owe A. C.
White the greatest debt of all.

(4) Castling. On the analogy of the P × P *e.p.* convention, Castling in problems would be permitted only if it can
be proved that neither the K nor R in question have moved
in the hypothetical game. As a matter of fact, there is no
possible position in which this can be proved, and, on this
argument, Castling should be ruled out of serious problems.
The majority of composers appear to fall in with this view,
but there is a fairly strong minority that upholds the manoeuvre. Whether the student takes the "Aye" or the "No"
side of this question, my advice to him is to avoid publication
of problems where *White* Castling would affect the real
solution, unless his admission of the manoeuvre is clearly
understood by all his readers. In the case of a possibility
of *Black* Castling as a defence, it would be as well to provide
a successful reply, whether the composer believes in allowing
the manoeuvre or not. A number of problems have been
composed which overcome the dilemma confronting a solver,
when he sees a K and R on their original squares, by
containing inherent evidence that one or other of these
pieces must have moved in the hypothetical game. No. 4
is the simplest example known of the Black "Can't Castle"
theme. Its composer, Sam Loyd (1841-1911) is the most
original genius of the problem art, and a king of puzzles of
all kinds. The Pony Puzzle, the Fourteen-Fifteen Puzzle,
"Get off the Earth," and Pigs-in-Clover, are some of his
familiar inventions.

9

No. 4 "CAN'T CASTLE" THEME

S. Loyd.   Musical World, 1859

Mate in 2

Black has just played, and it is quite evident, since the P's are on their original squares, that either his K or R must have moved.   Accordingly, after 1. Q – R1, Castling, which would "bust" the solution, is not a permissible defence.   As an example of a *White* "Can't Castle," see No. 152 in this book.

The four rules described above contain the only absolute conditions for the existence of a problem.   All the rest is a matter of taste, and in proceeding to deal in detail with the artistic principles of the modern two-move problem, I am quite sure that some of them will change.   Some *are* changing under our eyes; a healthy sign, for a standardised type of art cannot live long.

CHAPTER II

DEFINITIONS

A few definitions should be read before studying diagram No. 5.

Key Move, or *Key*, for short—White's first move, which solves the problem.

Cook. An alternative Key, not intended by the composer. In fact, an unlucky accident due to human fallibility. A problem with more than one Key is said to be "cooked." This term is sometimes applied also to an impossible position, or one with no solution.

Defence. A Black move that defeats the threat.

Try. A plausible first move that nearly, but not quite, solves the problem.

Variation. A Black move, in combination with the White mate following. Distinct variations depend on the White mates; if a dozen Black moves are followed by the same reply, this usually counts as one variation only. One of the chief aims of the modern problem is to get as many variations as possible, provided they display strategy and grow naturally out of the position.

Dual. A choice of two White moves, following a particular Black move. According to the standards of some Schools, in an ideal problem White should never have such a choice; he should be compelled to play in one way only, whatever Black does. Duals are flaws, which invalidate the variation in which they occur. A Cook may be regarded as a first-move Dual, spoiling the complete variation play, and therefore, in effect, the whole problem. Composers differ widely in their opinions on Duals. Some, if a Dual happens to occur in a variation that they consider to be unimportant, do not attempt to prevent it. Others will put on small Black force for that purpose, and others again will go to all lengths to cut it out. Undoubtedly the tendency grows to disregard them, unless they occur in important lines. In themselves, Duals differ in degree of virulence. In a *Minor Dual*, both possibilities for White are separately forced on him by other Black moves. In a *Major Dual*, one (or both) of the lines cannot be *compelled* in any part of the solution. A Major Dual therefore involves waste strategy and is the more objectionable.

Triple. A choice of three moves for White, following a particular Black move. Naturally, it is considered a rather worse flaw than a Dual, and has the same division into major and minor. So we have *Quadruples*, etc., and eventually, when the derivatives from the Latin numerals fail, Multiples. The term *Dual*, by the way, has also a loose general use for all sorts of White choices.

Threat. A Key definitely intending a particular mate.

A Double Threat. One that threatens two distinct mates.

Flight Square or Flight. A square to which the Black K can move.

Set Mate. A mate prepared in answer to a particular Black move, *before the key is made.*

King's Field. The squares next the K; in number, from three, when he is cornered, to eight, when he is in the open, as in the next diagram.

No. 5 THREAT

Mate in 2.

The full solution is given in a convenient form.

Key: Q—KR2. Threat: 2. P—K4. Variations:

Black	White	Black	White
1	2	1	2
P×P	Kt×KP	P—Kt4	Q—R7
P—Q4	Q—K5	P—Kt6	Q—R3
Kt—B6	Kt×P	R—B5	Q×R

Another way to write this out would be to omit "Threat:. 2. P – K4," and put after the variations "1. Any other. 2. P – K4."

The *Key*, by protecting B4, releases the White KP, which makes a *threat* of P – K4 mate. Black has six *defences*, nearly all of which are of the simplest kind, forcing as many White mates. These constitute the *variation* play. First, he may capture the threat piece by 1. P × P, which enables White to recapture. Next 1. P – Q4 protects the threatened square, but gives up guard of K5. Similarly 1. Kt – B6 and 1. R – B5 cover White's K4 square, but leave other squares unprotected, which White promptly occupies. By 1. P – Kt4 and P – Kt6 Black defends himself in an indirect manner, making *flight squares* or *flights* for his K, but *opening gates* for the White Q. The second of these, defends in a double manner, for it shuts off the White Q control of B4, so that 2. P – K4 would not be mate, apart from the reply K – Kt5. There is a *Triple* in the problem. After 1. R – R8 (and several other moves) White can play either 2. P – K4, Q – B4 or Q – KB2, each delivering mate. Notice that the last of these can never be forced on White, making this a *Major* Triple; I may add that 2. Q – B4 has not this effect, for it is not distinct from 2. Q × R after 1. R – B4, being *a move of the same piece to the same square*, which does not usually constitute a distinct mate. Besides the Triple, there is a Dual after 1. Kt anywhere except to B6, by 2. P – K4 or Kt × P. Both these mates are forced on White by other Black moves, as the solution shows, so that this is a *Minor* Dual. You may notice that after 1. R – B7, there is also a dual by 2. Q × R or P – K4 ; and after 1. R – K8, by 2. Q – B4 or Q – B2. But both these are fully included in the Triple, and are accordingly not counted as *distinct* Duals.

Nothing more remains to be said on the definition of Duals in the two-mover (though in Chapter X, I deal with them from the aesthetic standpoint) except that a choice of Q or R, or of Q or B, by a P giving mate by promotion, is not usually considered to constitute a Dual (see No. 18).

As an example of a *Cook*, look at 1. Kt × P ch in No. 5. Black must reply either Kt × Kt or K – K4, when White plays 2. Q – B5 mate. This, of course, ruins the problem. If it had been a serious attempt at composition, a Black P would have been placed on QKt3. A *Try* in No. 5 is Q – KKt2 with the *double threat* of Q – K4 or Q – Q5. Black has only two replies, R – B6 or Kt – B6; this is therefore a fairly " near " Try.

Set Mate. Before the key is made in No. 5, Q – B2 is *set*, or already prepared, in reply to R along the rank, or R – B7.

Problem No. 6, though deliberately adapted from No. 5, is of a totally different type.

Mate in 2

Key: Q—KR2.

Black	White	Black	White
1	**2**	**1**	**2**
P×P	Kt×P(K3)	P—Kt4	Q—R7
QKt any	Kt×QP	P—Kt6	Q—R3
KKt any	Q—KB2	P×Kt	P—K4
P—K5	Q—B4		

The omission of any threat in the solution is significant. The Key in fact is a *waiting-move*, creating a *Block* position. Black has no attack to defend, but unfortunately he has to move, and in doing so must expose himself to mate in one way or another. Any problem (of any length) must be either of this type (called a *Waiter* or Block) or of the Threat type, illustrated by No. 5. The Block problem can be sub-divided into two clearly marked kinds:—

(1) The Block of the Black force is complete before the Key, which merely waits for Black to commit himself. (Complete Block.)

(2) The Block is incomplete until the Key is made. (Incomplete Block.)

The Threat Problem comprises the following varieties:—

(1) The position may be a complete Block, but the Key is actually a threat. The whole point of this type is the deception caused by the Block feature, the solver naturally suspecting a waiting Key. (Complete Block-Threat or generally, Block-Threat.)

(2) Similarly, we can have an Incomplete Block-Threat, where nearly all Black's moves are provided for, and the deception is considerable, if not so convincing as in the Complete Block-Threat.

Examples:—No. 6 shows the Incomplete Block, the Key waiting and providing mates for four Black moves, P – K5, P × P, P – Kt4, and P – Kt6.

In No. 7, given below, I have varied No. 6 to Complete Block form, and at the same time have utilised the diagram to illustrate a well-known type of *Impossible Position*.

No. 7 COMPLETE BLOCK AND IMPOSSIBLE POSITION

Mate in 2

The solver will find that in answer to every one of Black's moves a mating reply is " set," or prepared before the Key, and White has merely to find a waiting move. The Key is K – B6, which still waits for Black to commit himself and identifies the Problem as a Complete Block before and after the Key. Notice some Tries: K elsewhere, defeated by check from one of the Black Kt's; B – R5 or Q – Kt4, met by P – Kt3; Q to R5 or R7, by Kt×B. Now, why is the position impossible, and the problem accordingly ruined? The answer lies in the eight Black P's, which, examination will show, must have made no less than eleven captures to arrive at their present position—that on B7 for instance must have come from QR2, capturing five units on the way. There are now six White pieces on the board, so that only ten have been put in the box. Q.E.D.

No. 8 BLOCK-THREAT

H. D'O. Bernard. Devon and Exeter Gazette, Jan. 1918

Mate in 2

No. 8 is a Complete Block, for, on examination of the Black moves, we find the following set play:

Black	*White*
1	**2**
Q×B or R×R	Q×Q or R
Q or R else	B×Q or R×R
P—Kt6	P×P

The Key is P – B4, *threatening* P × P. If either Black P captures (*en passant* or directly), the White Q recaptures. Other Black moves are answered as in the set play. The two captures by the Black P's, with the replies, constitute *Added* Variations. The threat, 2. P × P, is of course a new mate, but is not generally counted as " added," in the strict technical use of the word.

No. 9 INCOMPLETE BLOCK-THREAT

B. Harley. Globe, April 1913

Mate in 2

The above Problem is not a complete Block before the Key, for no mate is set in answer to 1. B×B, R. on file, P – KKt6 or QP moves. There is, however, about enough set play to mislead a solver for a little time into thinking the Key may be a waiting move, a deception which is the *raison d'etre* of the type of problem. Actually it is Q – K2, threatening 2. K – B2. Classifying the play, we have 1. K × P, allowing 2. R × P, as an added variation; while two other defences lead to *changed mates;* for instance:

1. B – Q5 ch 2. K – Q2 instead of B × B ; 1. R – B4 2. K – Q3, instead of KKt × KtP.

In the Incomplete -Block Threat, it is very important that the changed mates should follow prominent Black moves which catch the solver's eye, such as B – Q5 ch in No. 9; there would be little point in changing the mate after such obviously innocuous moves as P – KKt6.

Note that the White K and Q form what is called a *Direct Battery*. A *Battery* indicates two pieces on the same line as the crucial spot that is aimed at. When the front piece moves, the gun behind comes into action. Here the Q is the gun, and as her aim is at the Black K, the Battery is *Direct;* if aimed at a square in his field, it would be *Indirect*

No. 10 INCOMPLETE BLOCK-CHANGE

F. B. Feast. British Chess Magazine, Oct, 1918

Mate in 2

Every Black move is provided with a mating reply except R – K4, which by cutting off the guard of White's QB on Q6, paralyses the Kt on B8. The Key is B – R6, with the reply B – Kt7 following 1. R – K4, a mate that is also substituted (introducing the change element) for 2. KKt – Kt6, in reply to any move of the R on its file, except R – K2 or 5. Not only this, but a new mate is introduced by 1. K – B3, 2. Q × R, illustrating the added mate idea, as in No. 8.

We now come to the last of the big groups into which the two-mover can be divided: the Complete Block both before and after the Key, which changes one or more mates: that is, the Complete Block-Change, or, as I have christened it for short, the Mutate. No. 11 is a beautiful example.

No. 11 BLOCK-CHANGE OR MUTATE

P. H. Williams. Pittsburg Gazette 1911

Mate in 2

The Black moves should be studied first, when we see that after KKt any, we have R – B5; after QKt any, B – Q6; and after P – B4, B × Kt — that is, a Complete Block exists. No threat Key will work, though there are near tries by B × P, defeated by Kt × QP; or B – Q8 Kt – Q3! or P – K5 QKt any! and so on. The Key is the surprising move R – R4, still waiting for Black to commit suicide, and thus differing essentially from the Block-Threat. It will be useful to put out in parallel columns the set and the actual play:

	Set	Actual
1. Kt – KB6	2. R – B5 or Kt – R3 or K2	2. Kt – R3
Kt × KP	R – B5 or Kt – K6 or Kt – Q3	Kt – K6
KKt else	R – B5	P – Kt5
P – B4	B × Kt	KtP × P
QKt any	B – Q6	B – Q6

There are two changed mates, while the Triples in the set play following 1. Kt – KB6 and Kt × KP are eliminated. The Mutate has sprung into amazing popularity in the last twenty years, and a later chapter will deal more fully with this and the other forms of problems in which changed play is met, the Block-Threat and Incomplete Block-Threat.

To sum up the main types of the two mover:—we have
A. Threats.
   (1) Block-Threat.   (No. 8)
   (2) Incomplete Block-Threat.   (No. 9)
   (3) All others.
B. Blocks.
   (1) Incomplete Block (made complete by Key)   (No. 6)
   (2) Complete Block (both before and after Key)   (No. 7)
   and special cases of (1) and (2) in which some of the set mates are changed, giving
   (3) Incomplete Block-Change.   (No. 10)
   (4) Complete Block-Change or Mutate.   (No. 11)

CHAPTER III

THE KEY

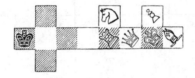

It is quite true that variation play is, in ninety-nine cases out of a hundred, the soul of a problem, or (to put it more materially) the main course of the solver's banquet, but the Key is the cocktail that begins the proceedings, and if it fails in piquancy the following dinner is not so satisfactory as it should be.

A rough definition of a good Key is a move that is the last, or one of the last, moves that an average player of the game would consider. Accordingly, bad Keys are those that appear obvious to him. For example, checks, captures and similar restrictions of the Black forces are, in general, inferior beginnings. Since the attention of a solver is called so critically to the Black K's position, a Key that deprives him of a flight contains a weakness; and prevention of outstanding Black defences, such as checks to the White K, capture or pin of important Black force, or shutting them out of play, are all bad features. I should explain that a piece is *pinned*, when it is on the line of its K, and cannot move off that line, without the illegality of exposing him to check. A question that often puzzles beginners at chess may be answered here. Can a pinned piece deliver mate? It can, in certain circumstances, for which the reader is referred to the remarks on No. 21.

The aggressive element in a Key may be counter-balanced, and indeed quite outweighed, by other considerations. A particular flight may be taken from the Black K, but another, sometimes several, may be given him in exchange. A capture of an insignificant Black unit, such as a P, may often be excused if it is balanced by some apparent advantage to the losing side, and in special cases (such as the self-pinning theme, shown in No. 19) is actually the best possible Key. Even a checking Key, if it comes as a surprise and leads to piquant play (as in Nos. 18 and 39) may be excellent.

I shall deal first with openings whose merits lie in the grant of greater comparative freedom to Black, either in counter-attack, general play or in units of force. Under this heading come Keys that allow Black to check the White K, that give the Black K flight squares, that sacrifice, pin, or otherwise appear to put out of play prominent White force, and that unpin or otherwise bring into play strong Black force. These we may call "Gift Keys," as contrasted with those that restrict Black force, or aim at a definite strategem without giving up any apparent advantage; and with neutral Keys, which merely threaten an obvious mate, or wait for Black to commit himself.

A fine Gift Key, such as is found in No. 12, often combines several of the factors mentioned above.

No. 12 SPECTACULAR KEY

A. J. Fink. Pittsburg Gazette Times 1914

Mate in 2

Key R—K2

Threat B—K6

if 1 K×R ch, 2 R—Q2
if 1 P×R,   2 Q—B7
and other variations

The Key gives a flight square to the Black K (incidentally sacrificing the QR in a second way) and allows Black a check to the bargain. Also the Key piece is offered to the Black P, with a surprising journey by the White Q following.

In my opinion, the points of Gift Keys may be graded in the following order of increasing merit:

(a) Sacrificial.
(b) Giving flights.
(c) Self-pinning of White force.
(d) Unpinning Black force.
(e) Allowing Black checks.

The Key of a Mutate, changing set mates, is *ipso facto* good, but is also subject to the canons set out above, and its quality may be enhanced or tarnished by plus or minus features.

Now to deal with my list in detail.

(a) Each sacrifice, to be thematic, must introduce a separate mate. It is no use putting White force *en prise*, if its capture has no effect at all on the variation play. Moreover, unless the sacrificial play can be done very neatly and with some subtlety, this typical game manoeuvre is hardly worth building into a theme, though an *individual* offer of a piece frequently occurs in modern problems, with good effect.

No. 13 SACRIFICIAL KEY

B. G. Laws. Northern Figaro 1888

Mate in 2

Key R—Q6

Threat: 2. Q×R

Black	White
1	2
K×R	Q—QB7
R×R	Kt—Kt4
B×R	Q—Kt7

The other variations are well worth working out, but I shall not give them here, nor generally any lines except those that illustrate the particular theme in question. Note that the White B and Kt form an *Indirect* Battery, trained upon Q4 square, opened up after 1 R×R. Compare No. 9, where a Direct Battery is shown.

A more intensive version is below.

No. 14 SACRIFICIAL KEY

M. Marble. La Stratégie 1908

Mate in 2

Key B—K4.   Threat Q×P

Black	White
1	2
K×B	R—B4
Q×KB	R—B2
QR×B	R—B1
KR×B	Kt—B5
KKt×B	Kt—K6
QKt×B	KR—Q3
P×B	Q—Q8

A sevenfold sacrifice of one piece, each capture yielding a different mate. Such intensive treatment of an idea constitutes a *Task Problem*, when the composer tries to achieve a new record in a particular theme. It is possible to offer more than one unit by the Key, but probably the only reasonable way of making this theme effective is by the multiple offer of a particular piece, as in the last two problems. The maximum number of sacrifices (the *extreme* Task) is ten, but the following position contains the greatest number of *distinct variations*, introduced by the capture of a single White unit.

No. 15 MULTI-SACRIFICE KEY
M. Marble (and others). Chess Amateur 1913

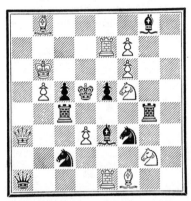

Mate in 2

Key Kt—Q4.   Threat R—Q8

It is a good exercise to examine the result of the captures of the Key piece; eight different mates result, 2. P × R following both B × Kt and KP × Kt. Strictly speaking, therefore, this is an eight-fold sacrifice.

The last three problems all combine Self-Block (see Chapter V) as the main interest, with Sacrificial Keys. I shall just mention other combinations, following the arrangement of the subject in *Simple Two-Move Themes* by F. B. Feast and A. C. White. Sacrifice to the Black K is excluded.

(1) Mate by recapture: see No. 78, 1. P × R 2. Q × P.
(2) Decoy of Black, from guard of a square: No. 13, 1. B × R
2. Q – Kt7. (The unguard of Kt7 is combined with Self-Block.)

(3) Decoy of Black from interposal: No. 14, 1. QR × B 2. R – B1 (with Self-Block).

(4) Decoy of Black from Pin of White: No. 114, 1. Q×P ch 2. R – Q3.

(5) Decoy of Black to Self-Pin: No. 97, 1. Kt × Kt ch 2. R – Q4 (the capturing Kt being pinned).

(6) Vacation by Black of a square, for occupation by the mating unit, which can only be a P. (No example in the book.)

(7) Vacation by Black of a line of White attack: No. 12, 1. P × R 2. Q – B7.

(8) Vacation by Black of a line of mate: No. 14, 1. P × B 2. Q – Q8 (with Self-Block).

(9) Vacation by Black of a line of guard: No. 13, 1. R × R 2. Kt – Kt4 (the White Q now holding K4).

(10) Vacation by Black of a line of Pin: No. 97, 1. Kt×Kt ch 2. R – Q4, the Black Q being left pinned, whereas it is the Black Kt's Pin that brings it under heading (5).

(11) Interference Sacrifices: No. 32.

This list is added for completeness. Several of the terms used have not yet been defined, and I suggest that the reader should leave them alone for the present. Hardly any of the divisions seem to admit of repetitive treatment in variations, and I conclude that Self-Block and Self-Pin are about the only suitable devices to be combined with a Sacrificial Key, for theme-building purposes. The student must be warned that he is very unlikely to do anything novel in sacrificial themes. However attractive it may appear to him, Sacrifice, *by itself*, is considered a comparatively weak and uninteresting form of problem strategy, and its proper use should be in conjunction with deeper ideas, to which it can add the charm of surprise.

(b) *Flight Giving Keys.*

Here again, the pure task of allowing the Black K a large number of outlets has been so intensively studied, that little remains to be done, and, as with sacrifice, one or two flights only will often combine with and enhance the value of fine strategy, and make a more interesting problem than the piling up of loopholes for the K.

No. 16 FLIGHT-GIVING KEY
S. Loyd. N.Y. Chess Association 1892

Mate in 2

Key Q—R1

Threat Q—K1

Black	White
1	2
K—K5	Q—Q4
K else	R—Kt2

There is very little variety here, and what there is follows moves by the Black K, a usual feature of the multi-flight Key. The success of the problem lies wholly in the surprising opening, which gives the Black K an entirely new line of deployment. A favourite theme, depending on moves by this piece, is the Star-Flight, in which he can move out diagonally in all four directions. The Key usually gives from one to three of these flights, though the task of giving all four has been achieved.

No. 17 STAR-FLIGHT THEME
A. G. Corrias. Good Companion Folder 1917

Mate in 2

Key P—Q6, waiting

Black	White
1	2
K—B1	B—B5
K—K1	Q—K7
K—K3	Q—B5
K—B3	B—R4

The Miniature effect is the best point, for the Key, although it gives two thematic flights, takes away B2 from the K. It may be called a "Give and Take" Key, with a small credit balance. In this problem each K move leads to a different mate, almost a *sine-qua non* in flight-giving themes.

Finally we come to the "extreme task" or record aspect of such Keys. I have lately been shown, by A. G. Stubbs, a checking Key that gives no less than seven flights to the Black K, but the same mate occurs after each of his moves; the following problem, where six outlets are given, has a great deal of interesting play.

No. 18 MULTI-FLIGHT KEY
Ua Tane. Good Companion Folder 1918

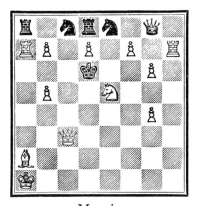

Mate in 2

Key   Kt—B4 ch.

Black	White
1	2
K—B2	KtP × Kt (Q)
K × P	P—B8 (Kt)
K—K2	BP × Kt(Q)
K—K3	P × Q (Q)
K—Q4	Q—K5
K—B4	R—KR5

This is a case where a checking Key can be very well condoned, owing to its complete unexpectedness and the six variations that it produces. You may notice, in going over the mating moves, that the White P's have options of promotion on three occasions; for instance after 1 K – B2, 2 KtP × Kt, becoming Q or R, will work. This, as pointed out in Chapter II, is not held to constitute a Dual, the R's powers being fully included in the Q's, but if the P could choose such essentially different pieces as a Q *or Kt*, a Dual would then arise.

(c) Self-pinning of White force by the Key is rather a rare feature, and, to be thematic, should lead to variations in which Black unpins the Key piece, allowing it to give different mates. Self-pinning can be done in various ways, i.e., by capture of a Black unit, by a move of the White K, or by taking one of two White pieces off the pin-line. No. 19 illustrates the first of these methods, No. 20 the second, and No. 21 the last.

No. 19 SELF-PINNING KEY BY CAPTURE

A. Bottacchi. Good Companion Folder, May 1919

Mate in 2

Key Q × QP.   Threat Q × Q

The White Q is unpinned by various moves of the Black Q, giving mate on the squares QR5, Kt5, B5 and B6, while 1 B – Q2 unpins her by interference, allowing 2 Q – Kt7. There is clearly no demerit in a capture Key here, as the balance of mobility is altered in Black's favour; the strongest White unit is greatly constrained at the cost of a blocked P.

No. 20 SELF-PINNING KEY BY K MOVE

G. Heathcote. Norwich Mercury 1907

Mate in 2

Key K—K5.

Threat K—Q4

Black	White
1	2
Q × P	Q × Q
Q—QR2	Q—B5
Kt—K6	Kt × B
R—R1 etc.	B—Kt4
B—R5	R × B
B—KB7	R—KB5

In this fine Task problem, the White K walks into no less than four pins, all of which are released by defences to the threat and result in distinct mates.

C. Promislo. Good Companion Folder, Oct. 1917

Mate in 2

Key R—K6

Threat Q—K5

Black	White
1	2
Kt—Q4	Q—Q6
B—Q4	Q—B8
B—B4	Q—B2

The threat is a correct mate, although the White Q
remains pinned. There are no exceptions whatever to the
rule that a pinned piece (the Black Q is here under review)
must not move, exposing its K to check. The logic is perfect,
for if after 2 Q – K5 ch Black could play Q×Q ch, *his* K
would be the first to be captured. (See p. 22).

(d) Unpinning of Black by the Key can be done either by
withdrawal of the pinning piece or interposal on the pin line,
the second method being the more subtle. For the Key to
be thematic, it is necessary that the unpinned Black unit
should provide several variations.

No 22 UNPINNING KEY BY INTERPOSAL

B. Harley. Pittsburg Gazette Times, Feb. 1914

Mate in 2

Key P—B4

Black	White
1	2
R—K4 ch	P×R
R—K5	P—K3
R×KP	P—B5
R—B6	P×R
R else	P—K4

This Complete Block with added variety is a hideous-looking object, somewhat excused by the five new mates (all given by P moves) that follow release of the R.

No. 23 is an excellent specimen of mixed Self-Pin and Unpin in the Key, a theme that has received much attention in the last few years.

No. 23 SCHÖR THEME DOUBLED

J. H. Barrow. Grantham Journal, Spt. 1927

Mate in 2

Key Q×BP. Threat R×P

If 1 Kt—Q4, 2 Q×QP ; if 1 Kt—B7, 2 P—Q3

Each of these two variations exemplifies the elaborate Schör Theme. The Key simultaneously pins two White units (Q and P) and unpins a Black unit (Kt). This Kt in turn unpins each of the White units, allowing it to mate. The Self-Pins are of distinct kinds, by capture and by removal of White force, so that the main strategic ideas of Nos. 19, 21 and 22 are all displayed in No. 23.

Unpinning Keys usually occur as waiting moves (as in No. 22), when they merely add variations, or as threats which allow Black strong counter-attacks. No. 26, given in the next section, is an example of this second species.

(e) Keys allowing Black checks have, from their brilliant effect, for many years been popular, and the idea that White, the attacking party, should allow his own K to be attacked appears to be a paradox that appeals particularly to the novice. This little bit of chess jujitsu can be performed by various devices: (1) The White K moves directly into danger. (2) He is exposed by one of his subordinates which leaves the check line, or opens a path for a Black piece. (3) The Key unpins a Black piece. (4) A flight is given to the Black K, which by moving delivers discovered check. (5) Miscellaneous.

The following diagrams, with the Black check variations given in full, illustrate the processes given above, and not much further comment is necessary. All but one contain at least two checking variations, as they should, to render their Keys thematic; No. 26 has only one check, but that is a double blow, illustrating a rare theme, which was worth doing once, but possibly not again, for it does not combine well with other strategy. The Black Check Theme came into its own at the beginning of the century, and for a considerable time held the field in popular favour. Chess problem ideas are very like the fashions in other arts. They run a meteoric course, their finest expressions sweeping the tourney-board (even the severe judges of such competitions come under the hypnotic spell) and are suddenly dropped when a novelty appears. Nevertheless, the Black Check remains a favourite to this day, and much remains to be done in its genre.

No. 24 KEY ALLOWING CHECK BY WHITE K MOVE

W. A. Shinkman. Brentano's Monthly, July 1880

Mate in 2

Key K—K3

Threat Kt—B3

If 1 B—R3 ch 2 P—B4

If 1 R—K2 ch 2 Kt—K4

(Incidentally, an example of *Mutual Interference* of Black R and B, dealt with in Chapter V.)

No. 25 KEY ALLOWING CHECK BY REMOVAL FROM CHECK LINE

C. G. Watney and B. Harley. Chess Pie, No. 1, 1922

Mate in 2

Key R × P.

Double Threat
Kt—B5 or Kt6.

Black	White
1	2
Kt × R ch	Kt—Kt6
Kt—B7 ch	Kt—B5
Kt—B3 ch	R—Kt6
Kt—Kt4 ch	R—Q3

The mate, R—Kt6, is known as a "*Switchback*," the Key piece returning to its starting point.

No. 26 KEY ALLOWING CHECK BY UNPIN

H. E. & J. Bettmann. Quebec Chronicle 1882

Mate in 2

Key Q—R5

If 1 Kt×Kt double ch, 2 K—B3

No. 27 KEY ALLOWING CHECK BY GIVING FLIGHTS

T. C. Evans. Observer, January 1923

Mate in 2

Key Kt—QB3. Threat Kt—K6

If 1 K—B3 ch,   2 Kt—K6

If 1 K—B5 ch,   2 Kt×B

Under the miscellaneous section, we get Keys that move out of the path of the Black unit predestined to check; those that mobilise a blocked Black piece, and the like, which hardly need an explanatory diagram.

The last fifteen examples (Nos. 13 to 27) have shown, in essentials, nearly every kind of Key that can increase Black's comparative power or mobility. It is, of course, quite possible to give freedom to Black by other means than allowing his K flights, or unpinning his subjects; a simple clearance of a square or line may have a pointed effect, as in No. 28.

No. 28 KEY FREES BLACK BY LINE CLEARANCE

A. C. White. Westminster Gazette 1917

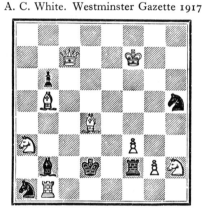

Mate in 2

Key P – Kt4, allowing R × Kt, when 2 Q × R follows. This is a Complete Block position, both before and after the Key, with an added mate. There is a neat point in the fact that P – Kt3 will not work, as it shuts off the Q from her prey.

The mobility of an important White piece can be reduced, or its direction changed, by square or line obstruction, without the devices of sacrifice, self-pinning, etc. The next position exemplifies what is called "Masking a White line of attack."

No. 29 KEY OBSTRUCTS OR *MASKS* A WHITE PIECE

Mrs. W. J. Baird. Times Weekly, Oct. 1919

Mate in 2

Key Kt—B3.   Threat Kt × KtP
If 1 P—Q6, 2 Q—K5

This is a Block-Threat, in which the Q's control of K3 is required in the set mates. The Key masks this control, also giving a flight on the crucial rank, and all the true White play is quite new.

In general, White Masking Keys lend themselves most readily to the change-mate theme.   No. 137 is an example, in which three new mates arise from moves by the Black B, instead of the set Q—KR8.

An example is given of the special kind of Line Masking known as the "Anti-Bristol," in which the Key piece moves *along* the "critical" line, that between the White Q and B. The student will find it useful, in order to understand the title "Anti-Bristol," to refer at once to the Bristol theme of No. 34 (page 42) in which the Key R moves *away from* the Q, clearing a path for her; whereas in No. 30 the Key B moves *towards* his Q, preventing her from crossing over to QKt7.

No. 30 WHITE ANTI-BRISTOL

T. Warton. Manchester City News, April 1919

Mate in 2

Key B—K4

preventing 2 Q—QKt7 after 1 B—Kt3, and substituting 2 Q×QB.

We now come to Keys that do not aim at giving an apparent advantage to Black, either in strength or mobility. The merit of such Keys must lie in their subtlety or peculiarity. A favourite device is the "Ambush" in which the key piece attacks *indirectly*. No. 31 is a fine example.

No. 31 AMBUSH KEY

P. F. Blake. Observer, July 1920

Mate in 2

Key Q—Kt1

Threat Kt—Q3

The White Q gives up a commanding position, where she controls the maximum of five squares in the Black K's field, and sneaks off to a spot from which she holds only one. Her ambush (by Indirect Battery) is against QKt5 square, which is necessarily shut off from her KB by the threat, Kt—Q3.

No. 32 shows a thoroughgoing obstruction of Black's strongest defensive force, with a multiple threat (2 R any), but it is extremely piquant, and the Black check introduced (1 P × Kt ch, 2 R—QR4) is a pretty feature.

No. 32 KEY OBSTRUCTS BLACK (NOWOTNY)
N. M. Gibbins. Leeds Mercury, Aug. 1901

Mate in 2

Key Kt—Kt2.   Threat R any
If 1 R × Kt, 2 R—B2; if 1 B × Kt 2 R—Q4

This stratagem, in which a Black R and B are cut off at their point of juncture, with the result that capture of the key piece induces mutual interference, is called the Nowotny Theme, from the composer of an early example.

Before the reader comes to the next example, some definitions are necessary.   A *Critical Square* denotes one that must be crossed by either a White or Black piece, before an offensive or defensive manoeuvre can be carried out successfully.

Such a move, getting rid of a critical objection, whether made by White as a Key (generally to avoid interference with another of his units) or by Black, in defending a threat, is called *Anticritical*. But when Black play *introduces* the critical objection, to his disadvantage, he is said to make a *Critical Move*.

No. 33 ANTICRITICAL KEY AND CRITICAL DEFENCES

B. Harley. De Schelde, Dec. 1926

Mate in 2

Key Q—R7. Threat Q—KB7
If 1 Q—B1, 2, or 3, 2 Kt—B5. If 1 Q—K5, 2 QKt—Q4

White intends, in certain circumstances, to mate by QKt —Q4, which, as the position stands, would cut off control of QB5 by his Q; therefore the Key piece must pass over this square, critical to White (the point is well underlined by the Try 1 Kt × P ch Q × Kt, 2 QKt – Q4 ch K – B4). The same square becomes critical to Black, after the defence Q – B1, 2 or 3, for quite another reason; White can then by Kt – B5 *shut off* the Q from interposal. A second square, White's Q4, also becomes critical to Black, in the defensive variation 1 Q – K5, when the Shut-Off again becomes effective. The Key, getting rid of White's objection to QB5 square, is therefore *Anticritical*, while the Black Q moves, introducing squares objectionable to herself, are Critical.

No. 34 CLEARANCE KEY

H. D'O. Bernard. Western Morning News, Nov. 1903

Mate in 2

Key R—QR1   If 1 K—B4.   2 Q—Kt1.

This may be called a Two-move Bristol Theme and is directly contrasted with the Anti-Bristol, No. 30. The Bristol Theme was invented by F. Healey in a famous three-mover that won first prize in a Composing Tourney of the British Chess Federation at that city in 1861. The theme includes a line-clearance, such as No. 34 exploits, and the absolute passivity and uselessness of the Key piece, after its expedition, is an essential part of the surprise. No. 34 is a Mutate, and the mate 2. P – K4, prepared for 1. K – B4, is very neatly changed by clearing the lowest line. Very similar strategy is found in No. 35, the difference lying in the fact that the White KB cannot go beyond the board to make room for his Q, after the only Black defence unprovided for, and has to *annihilate* himself.

42

No. 35 ANNIHILATION KEY
B. J. de C. Andrade. The Review, May 1924

Mate in 2

Key B—Kt8

If 1 Q×B, 2 Q×Q.

Although this Key puts a B *en prise*, it is essentially not a Gift Key, but a Line Clearance, providing for a particular Black move, Q – Kt1. A few other examples of Provision of various kinds are given below.

No. 36 PROVISION KEY
P. Klett. Schach Probleme, 1878

Mate in 2

Key R—Kt3

If 1 K—B3, 2 B—Q4

The square chosen by the R Key (instead of Kt4) provides for the Black *second move* defence, 2 Q – K4, in the main variation given above. It looks ahead, therefore, as far as is possible, and contains the curious feature of introducing the strategy which it defends. In fact, this is a Gift Key and a Provision Key in one. I should perhaps add that all Keys are, in a broad sense, provisional, and very many have a clear-cut object (such as, for one example, the completion of a block position). No. 36, however, seems to me to deserve its title by its peculiar longsightedness, and No. 37 by its quaint effect.

No. 37 PROVISION KEY. RED INDIAN THEME

F. Janet (after S. Loyd), British Chess Magazine, Sept. 1918

Mate in 2

Key B—KB8. Threat Q—R1
If 1 B×R, 2 B×Q

White intends to mate by Q – R1, and the trouble is, what is he to do against the palpable defence B × R? This long trail by a White piece, coming round at an angle to finish off the Black K, is picturesquely called the Red Indian or American Indian Theme.

No. 38 is a pretty little problem, with the point that the Key R allows and provides for a Black check. The effect is very similar to that of No. 36.

No. 38 PROVISION KEY

D. Mackay. Observer, May 1920

Mate in 2

Key R—K3

If 1 Q any (including
Q—Kt 2 ch) 2 R—QB3

Such violent openings as captures, purely for the sake of removing a Black defence (and not for the thematic self-pinning of White, as in No. 19) or checks, can rarely be effective, but as the art of the chess problem has many facets, and humour is one of them, No. 39, which has probably defeated as many solvers in its sixty-year existence as any other two-mover, will be enjoyed by most people.

No. 39 CHECKING KEY

S. Loyd. La Stratégie, Feb. 1867

Mate in 2

Key Q—KKt4 ch.

If 1 P—B4 2 P×P *e.p*

The position after 1 P – B4 is very curious, the Black K having no less than four flight squares, all taken away by the *en passant* capture. Compare the complex No. 18 with this simplicity.

It will not be necessary to give further examples of "neutral" Keys, that have no striking features, merely making a simple threat of mate, or completing a Block, as in Nos. 5 and 6, while the different devices that produce changed mates are dealt with in Chapter VIII. One small point may be added: generally speaking, a threat Key gains a little subtlety, if the intended mate is given by a unit other than the Key piece; similarly, a Key threatening mate by discovery (the opening of a Battery) indicates that two units must be watched by the solver. These, however, are not very important advantages, and are often, of course, impracticable. Such considerations bring us to the much-vexed question of difficulty in a Key.

Chess editors are well used to hearing the same problem described as "very difficult" and "very easy" by their solvers. Some happen to hit on the Key at once, and others are unlucky! Again, the finest strategic Keys, allowing multifarious Black checks, etc., will be the first to be tried by the expert (who would look for that very opening if the problem were his own composition) and about the last that would occur to the novice. You must fix your class of solver, before you can begin to measure "difficulty." Perhaps, taking all grades together, from him who has not learned his problem alphabet to the past master of the art, a complicated position with a quiet, non-committal sort of Key, and various plausible Tries, would get the highest average amount of failures. Difficulty, being so impossible to measure, is not directly aimed at by the modern composer, except for the special purpose of upsetting solvers' scores in a tourney, or as an occasional *jeu d'esprit*. At the same time, he is very pleased if his productions, after being worked up to the highest artistic finish, are found to contain some excellent Tries, defeated by a single and subtle Black defence, and he might occasionally sacrifice some final polish for this purpose.

CHAPTER IV

THEMES, BASED ON BLACK DEFENCES

The word "Theme" in connection with the two-mover is generally used to indicate repetition of a particular stratagem in several variations. Occasionally, a single variation of a complex kind may also make a theme (see No. 102), but I should prefer the word "idea" for such little jokes as Loyd's No. 39, or (say) a Mutate with one piquant changed mate. The last generation produced a large number of fine two-movers in which repetitive strategy was not found, or at any rate not prominent, the composer relying upon the effect of a nicely-blended set of unrelated variations. It is becoming more and more difficult to be sure of the essential originality of such positions, and we find the great modern composers, with a few outstanding exceptions, relying upon multiplying an idea in two, three or more variations.

In this chapter I am dealing with themes based on delib- erate Black Defences. Such elementary defences to a threat as capture or interference of the attacking White piece are to be seen in innumerable problems, but can hardly be made into a successful theme, while the retirement, by various outlets, of the Black K has been sufficiently shown in the Key-Flight examples. The more subtle defence of capture of a White unit, other than the threat piece, is hardly to be found as a theme outside the kind of multi-sacrifice idea of Nos. 14 and 15. The device of obtaining flights for the doomed K is quite amenable to theme form, more especially when the variation play depends on removal of the same Black piece. No. 40 illustrates this idea, with a well-known, not to say hackneyed struggle between a Black R and White P.

No. 40 DEFENCE BY OBTAINING FLIGHT

B. Harley. Reading Observer, Sept 1911

Mate in 2

Key B—K8. Threat B × Kt

Black	White
1	2
R × P	B—Kt5
R—B6	P × R
R—Q5	P—Q3
R else	P—Q4

Here the release of the Black R gives four variations, in the first of which the White B "switchbacks" to its initial position.

In No. 41 the play is richer and more interesting.

No. 41 DEFENCE BY OBTAINING FLIGHTS

C. Mansfield. Densmore Memorial, 1918-20

Mate in 2

Key Q—B1.

Threat Q—QKt1

Black	White
1	2
Kt × P (Q5)	B—R2
Kt × KP	B × Kt
Kt—Kt6	B—Kt5
Kt × either Pch	B × Kt

A duel, with five episodes, between the Black Kt and the White B.

As an example of flights obtained by different Black pieces, and therefore on distinct squares, we have No. 42.

No. 42 DEFENCE BY OBTAINING FLIGHTS

H. Fischer. Deutsches Wochenschach, Aug. 1919

Mate in 2

Key Kt—Kt4

Black	White
1	2
B any	Kt—K7
Kt any	Kt—B4
P—B6	Kt—K3
P—K6	Kt—B6

The Key threatens three mates, but there are no Duals, as every Black move forces a separate reply. It might be argued here that, as no play by the B or P's defeats *all* three threats, their moves are not strictly defences. I hold, however, that even in a Block, or waiting-move position, such devices as obtaining flights, checking the White K and some others, are of their essential nature defensive and may be so esteemed, provided they force a particular White reply.

Almost the simplest form of defence is the move of a Black unit to defend the mating square, either directly or by unmasking. It is the *raison d'etre* of most beginners' efforts, where the whole of the variation play arises from replies to the threat that remove guards on other squares, and so allow White to mate. By itself, this can hardly constitute a worthy theme, but in combination with other strategy it is frequently successful.

In No. 43, six variations follow moves by the Kt on K4, which unmasks the Black R upon the threat square, White's K3. Here we have, in addition to the simple theme, a mixture of Self-Interferences and Unpins by Black. Generally speaking, this kind of defence is best thematised by using, as here, one—or occasionally two—unmasking Black units to do the work.

No. 43 DEFENCE OF THREAT SQUARE BY UNMASKING

K. S. Howard and B. Harley. Observer, Aug. 1925

Mate in 2

Key Q × BP. Threat Kt—K3

Black	White
1	2
Kt—B3	R × B
Kt × R	P × Kt
Kt—Q6	R—Q4
Kt—B6	Q—Q6
Kt—B2	Q—Q4
Kt—Q2	B—Kt7

A special form of unmasking defence, analogous to White Clearance (see No. 34), clears a path for another Black piece to move *in the same direction*, and can only be shown by a double jump of a P, to allow a Q or R to follow it up: i.e. a P on (say) K2 moves to K4 to allow a R on K1 to protect K3 square. A single example has, no doubt, appeared in several problems, but there is hardly scope, in view of such restrictions of force, for a theme.

We now come to Defences which involve counter-attack on the White K: directly, by check, or indirectly, either by depriving him of flights (thus preventing him from discovering mate) or by pinning his assistants. Several examples of the Black Check Theme have already appeared in the chapter on Keys, but they were there considered only from the point of view of White's opening, and must now be dealt with as a Defensive Theme.

Any number of ideas can be based upon Black checks. The most obvious are based purely on multiplication of the manoeuvre, without regard to strategic finesse, such as the task theme of obtaining a record number, either by the whole Black force or by individual pieces. I have seen a two-move problem in which the White K underwent sixteen different checks, but I do not know if this is the maximum so far attained. Twelve checks by the Black Q have been done several times. In No. 44, a fine example, she has ten shies at the cocoanut.

No 44 BLACK QUEEN CHECKS
G. Heathcote and J. Scheel. Hampshire Post, 1915

Mate in 2

Key R—B8.

Threat Kt—QB4

The variations are self-evident

E. Millins has made a study of four *direct* checks by the Black Rooks, and a similar number by the Knights has often been done. Checks by *discovery* are, however, much more frequent in the modern problem, and five have been produced by a single R, B or Kt, and four by a P (the maximum possible). When all is said and done, there is little doubt that, apart from some extreme tasks, A. C. White's division of the Black Check Theme according to the nature of White's reply is the most satisfactory. His three sections are as follows :—

(1) Capture of the checking piece, which he calls "Direct Return Capture Check"

(2) Moving the White K (not capturing the checking piece), or "Royal Battery Check" and

(3) Interposing a mating piece, or "Cross-check."

(1) As a theme, the Direct Return Capture Check is not attractive; obviously it is the least subtle method of repelling a Black check and while examples occur as side lines throughout the problem domain, I doubt if any good composer has deliberately worked for them.

(2) The Royal Battery Check is a pretty device, but difficult of much repetition in a problem, and it is generally found as an isolated example combined with other strategic variations. No. 45 shows two such checks. The real task here, as set by C. Mansfield, was four discovered checks by a Black B, replied to by different moves of the White K; two other checks in No. 45, 1. B – K5 and K7 ch, are met by *capture* by the White K, and are therefore, by definition, not Royal Battery checks.

No. 45 ROYAL BATTERY CHECKS
J. K. Heydon. Good Companion Folder, May 1920

Mate in 2
Key P—K4

Black	White
1	2
B—Q8 ch	K—B4
B×B ch	K—B2

(3) Without any doubt at all, the Cross-Check is the most ingenious form of the Black Check Theme. The obvious squares of the attacker and the attacked, those on which the checking piece and the White K stand, are relegated to the background and the defence deploys *across* the critical line; hence the name. Moreover, the cumulative experience of a generation of composers proves that far richer incidental strategy can be worked into the Cross-Check defence than either of the others. I now give a masterly example of the pure theme.

No. 46 CROSS-CHECK

C. Mansfield. Good Companion Folder, March 1917

Mate in 2

Key B—K4. Threat Kt × Kt

Black	White
1	2
Kt × Kt ch	B—Q3
Kt—K4 ch	R—Q3
Kt × R ch	Kt—Q Kt5
Kt—Q7 ch	Kt—B4

Most problemists deem this the finest Cross-Checker ex- ant. The Key, unpinning the Black Kt and thus introducing the entire theme, also gives a flight, and is "such stuff as dreams are made on," to be obtained only a few times in a composer's career; the four variations yielded by the Black checks are all "stars," with subtle replies following Self-Block, Self-Pinning, and other strategy. There are five strategic lines, woven together in a magical manner: from K3 to K5, interrupted by the Key; QR6 to K2, opened up by the Key; QR4 to K4, opened by the Black checks (allowing 2. Kt – Kt5 in reply to 1. Kt × R ch, while 2. Kt – B4, an interruption of the line, becomes impossible); QKt8 to KB4; and QB1 to KB4, both of which yield Battery mates.

The problem may be used to illustrate an important point (to my mind) in the Black Check Theme, that has not been much emphasized by previous writers. That is, the desirability of making the attack on the White K *in itself* essential to the mate. Taking the four variations of No. 46, we see that if the White K were not checked (let us put him at home on K1) 1. Kt × Kt could be met by either B – Q3 or B × Kt. So 1. Kt – K4 would have a dual reply in R – Q3 or B3 ; and 1. Kt × R would yield to a fivefold option of the White Kt. In these three variations, the Black Check fixes the mate and prevents Duals. In the fourth variation, however, 1. Kt – Q7 forces Kt – B4 (to hold the KR) whether it delivers check or not; this variation lacks the essentiality of the counter-attack on the White K, and is not ideal.

The Cross-Check Theme can be sub-divided into many groups (a useful one is dependent on discovered checks by a particular Black piece, exemplified by the Kt in No. 46) but I have no space to give more positions here; the idea, in combination with other themes, will frequently appear later in the book. The reader should be quite clear that neither the Black Check nor the White reply *need* be given by discovery; all that is necessary for the theme is that the moving piece in the mate should interpose on the Black checking line.

The next strategic Black Defence to be dealt with is the Pin. A single specimen of paralysis of the White attack by this means is not uncommon in a problem, but the intensive theme is much more unusual than the Black Check Defence, and a good deal of unexplored ground remains. Pinning of a White unit can be done directly, that is, by the Black piece moving to the crucial line, or by discovery, and the two next problems illustrate each method.

No. 47 DIRECT BLACK PIN DEFENCE

G. Guidelli. Good Companion Folder, Nov. 1915

Mate in 2

Key R—KB5.

Threat R × QP

Black	White
1	2
Q—B4	Q—KR1
Q—QB5	P × Q
Q—B6	Kt × Q
R—B4	Kt × P(Kt6)
R—B7	Q × Q

No. 48 BLACK PIN DEFENCE BY DISCOVERY

J. C. J. Wainwright. Good Companion Folder, May 1914

Mate in 2

Key B—B8.
Threat Kt—Kt8

Black	White
1	2
P × B	Q × P
P—B3	Q—B3
P—B4	Q—QR1

(Compare No. 76, where a Black P is also the favoured piece)

In No. 47, there are five direct pins of the threat piece, yielding different mates, and in No. 48 all three moves of the Black QBP pin the White Kt by discovery, and force separate replies.

We now come to my last group of Black Defences, the Unpin. This device is most effectively carried out by interference on the pin line, the obvious resources of capturing the White pinning piece, or moving the Black K, not yielding themselves readily to thematic construction. A single example must suffice here, composed by the South American expert who was the first to make an extended study of the stratagem.

No 49 BLACK UNPIN DEFENCE
A. Ellerman. Good Companion Folder, July 1917

Mate in 2

Key Q—R4. Threat Q—K4

Black	White
1	2
B—K4	Q×P
Kt (Kt3)—K4	Kt—R4
Kt (Kt5)—K4	Kt—K3
P—K4	Q—Q7

The Black QP is unpinned by four pieces on the same square (which is a flight given by the Key). Usually the "Line" Unpin Theme is carried out upon several squares.

CHAPTER V

THEMES. BASED ON BLACK MISTAKES

In this chapter, I deal with themes arising from errors by Black which abandon strategic points, or obstruct, or pin his own force. Every Black move must, of course, be some kind of a mistake, whether active or passive. In Chapter IV, the composers' ideas are grouped around Black's efforts to improve his forlorn position; in the present one, they concentrate on certain peculiar effects, produced either by supine alternatives in a Block position, or by moves that attempt nothing more than the defeat of a threat.

Perhaps the most popular idea based on Black giving up strategic points is the Focal Theme, but it is rarely met with nowadays without the admixture of some deeper strategy. During the Victorian era, it was the mainstay of multitudes of problems, and one got rather tired of the feeble imitations of expert work that flooded chess columns. In the Focal Theme a Black piece "focuses" two lines, on some points of which White, by upsetting the focus, will mate. The Black unit may be a Q, R or B (a Kt or P can focus only *squares*) and any amount of different combinations are possible; usually, but not necessarily, the position is a Complete Block after the Key, so that any move of the critical piece gives up control of one of the mating squares that constitute the "foci." I give as an example a famous chestnut, still remembering the thrill of the Key.

No. 50 FOCAL THEME

S. Loyd. American Chess Nuts, 1868

Mate in 2

Key B—K5

This is a Block after the Key, which adds the mate P—B6 an opening of a double R Battery by a P that has been used in many problems) as the reply to 1. K × Kt. Here the Black Q "focuses" her K2 and QKt5 squares, which the White Kt also focuses. Moreover, she has two spare moves, Q – K5 and K8, which cover these spots from a different focus. The Key, however, neatly cuts off her intention of waiting for White to declare himself. In modern problems, the Focal idea is usually incidental to interference play, or some striking device, such as change of the focus by the Key. (See No. 136.) Otherwise, it remains a very useful method of "controlling" a Black unit (*i.e.* providing mates for all its moves) and is part of every composer's stock-in-trade.

Next, there is the "Open Gate" Theme, in which a Black unit, by moving, vacates a line for deployment of the mating piece. This, again, is by itself simple strategy and found usually as a side line. In No. 51, however, we have it worked up very nicely into a real thematic entity, every Black move except Kt – K2 opening a gate for White.

No. 51 OPEN GATE THEME

P. H. Williams. British Chess Magazine, 1893

Key Q—R8

The variations are all obvious, three paths being opened for the Q, and two for the R. These pieces may be said to exemplify masked *White* focal play, the Q, for instance, looking over the heads of the Black Kt's at the squares B8 and K5. Such "Open Gates" illustrate a particular form of what A. C. White calls "White – Black Clearance," Black clearing a line or square for the benefit of White. He uses the term *Black – White* Clearance, in cases where *White* clears for Black's apparent benefit, as shown already in several cross-check problems, and others. T. R. Dawson confines "Line-Clearance" to cases where the moving piece remains on the mating line. (See No. 34.) Where it goes off the line, as in every example in No. 51, he calls the movement a "Line-Evacuation."

The most frequent and elementary method of Black self-obstruction is the Self-Block, when a Black piece moves next his K, either depriving him of a flight square, or setting free a White unit. It should be distinctly understood that the crucial square must not be barred from the mated K by any other reason than the blocking piece; turning to No. 15, it will be seen that the variations QR × Kt, and BP × Kt, allowing Q × P and Q – Q6 respectively, are not true Self-Blocks, as the White Q covers her Q4 square in the mates, but that every other capture of the Kt (excluding that by the K, who cannot self-block himself!) is actually a Self-Block. The following position is without doubt the finest known exposition of the theme. The two composers, living as far apart as San Francisco and Tahiti, had a curious simultaneous experience, one dreaming the position and the other the Key; Ua Tane ("Mr." Ua, the name given by the natives to James F. Stimson) believes there was thought-transference at work, due to the operations of a friend, an amateur medium, who was shown the idea of the problem.

No. 52 SELF-BLOCK RECORD

A. J. Fink and Ua Tane. Good Companion Folder, July 1920

Mate in 2

Key R—B8

The eight self-blocking moves are:

Kt × P, QP × P, P – Q3, P – K3, BP × P, R – Q5, Kt – Q5 and Kt – B4. Two of them occur on Black's Q5 square, but yield distinct mates. The Key is a waiting move, almost always the case in extreme examples of this theme, and has the extraordinary merit of changing the mates after 1. QP × P from R – Q7 to R – Q8, and after 1. Kt × P from R × QP to Kt – B7; in fact this is a Mutate. The last-mentioned variation should be particularly noted; it involves a White Self-Interference, the QKt being able to interfere with the R's defence of QB6 square, by reason of the Self-Block. The "Self-Block with White Interference," as it is called, is a sort of "Combination Theme" idea, but may conveniently be dealt with here. In this theme, as the example below shows, the crucial square is protected by a White piece (which must be a Q, R, or B) whose cover of that square is cut off by the mating unit. No. 53 is an example of five White Interferences, with the special record features of four on one line, that extending from the White QP to the KR, and of four Self-Blocks, introducing the Interferences, on the same square.

No. 53 SELF-BLOCK WITH WHITE INTERFERENCE

B. J. de C. Andrade and B. Harley. Observer, June 1924

Mate in 2

Key B—B7. Threat R—Q6

Black	White
1	2
K Kt×P	Kt—B4
P×QP	P—B4
B×QP	P—K4
Q Kt×QP	B—K4
B—B3	Kt—Kt6

The four different captures of White's QP enable him to interfere with the guard of this square by his R in different ways, while 1. B – B3 allows the action of the other R to be cut off. The device for forcing 2. B – K4 after 1. QKt × P, by the pinning of White's KP, should be noted.

The next position was an entry in a Composing Tourney conducted by a Belgian chess magazine. It is the absolute record in White Interferences.

L. A. Issaeff. L'Echiquier. August, 1929

Mate in 2

Key Q—Kt7. Threat Q×BP

Black	*White*
1	2
P—QB3	Kt—B6
P—B4	R—Q6
Kt—B4	Kt—K7
QKt—Q5	P—K4
KKt—Q5	B—K4
P—K5	Kt—B4

The composer has combined two well-known devices, the double blocks by the Black QBP and the Kt moves to Q5 (for the second, compare No. 53) and has added the P – K5 variation. An extreme task has rarely been so beautifully achieved. Other kinds of White Interference (*i.e.* without Self-Block), including the special case of its Avoidance, are treated in Chapter VI. White Interference is a strange business. The composer seems to be afraid to take Black's part openly (as in such themes as Black Checks). He handicaps the winner in an insidious way, making him strive to overcome interferences by his own side. "Defend me from my friends," is White's prayer in this theme.

Returning to the Self-Block Theme *per se*, a great deal of fine work has been done in the way of experimenting with a particular Black piece. Examination will show that the maximum number of Self-Blocks that can be given by a Q, R, B, Kt or P, is respectively five, four, two, two and three, and all these tasks have been achieved. The Q maximum does not lend itself to neat treatment, and I therefore quote a position illustrating only three Self-Blocks by this piece, but in classic form.

No. 55 SELF-BLOCKS BY Q

G. Heathcote. Leisure Hour, 1900

Key Kt—Q6

Black	White
I	2
Q—Kt3	R—QB1
Q—B3	Kt×P
Q×Kt	R—QB3

Incidentally, 1. P × Kt makes another Self-Block, allowing the White Interference, 2. B – Q4.

As an example of two Kt's blocking their maximum of four squares (a popular theme, known as the "Horse-Block") we have No. 56 by a specialist on the subject.

No. 56 SELF-BLOCKS BY KTS (HORSE-BLOCK)
F. Janet. Observer, July 1924

Mate in 2

Key P—Q4

Threat Kt—B3

Black	White
1	2
K Kt × Kt	Q—Kt8
Q Kt × Kt	Q—Q R2
Kt—K3	R × BP
Kt—B5	R—Kt5

A fifth Self-Block, a pedestrian one this, occurs by 1. P × Kt, allowing 2. Q × KKt mate.

In No. 57 we have four Self-Blocks by two promoting Black P's—not a record, since five have been done by this force, and six are a possibility. I choose the position to illustrate, in addition, Self-Blocks of *distinct flights*, which have not appeared in my previous examples of the theme, and are rarely found in any large number in one problem.

No. 57 SELF-BLOCKS BY PAWN PROMOTIONS
C. G. Watney. Good Companion Folder, May 1920

Mate in 2

Key B—B4

Black	White
1	2
BP=Q	K Kt—B2
BP=Kt	Q—Q5
RP=Q ch	Kt—R2
RP=Kt	Kt—K3

An important group of themes is based on Black Self-Interference (often called Black Interference, simply) by which is understood the masking of the action of one Black piece by the move of another. In No. 32, the Nowotny Key shows White as the cause of obstruction, but it is evidently more subtle strategy to induce Black to cause his own downfall, either by defeating a threat or by the necessity of moving in a Block position. Some scattered examples of Black Self-Interference have already appeared, as in Nos. 24, 31, etc., and it has now to be considered as a theme. No. 58 shows the greatest number (eight) of such variations, leading to distinct White mates, so far attained.

No. 58 BLACK INTERFERENCE
B. Harley. Pittsburgh Gazette Times, Dec. 1916

Mate in 2

Key Q—K7. Threat Q—K5

Black	White	Black	White
1	2	1	2
R—K3	Q—R4	Kt—Kt 3	B×P
B—K3	Q×P	B—B6	Q—K3
Kt—K3	Q×R	Kt—Q6	R—B3
Kt—Q2	R—R4	Kt—B6	P—Kt3

The Key, as usual in extreme tasks, is poor, the White Q going from *en prise* to an aggressive position. To make the stratagem quite clear, take the first variation 1. R – K3; this allows 2. Q – R4, because the R interferes with the cover of his QKt5 square by the QB. Self-Interferences are called "objective" with regard to the moving Black piece, and "subjective" with regard to the unit interfered with. Thus, the above variation is an objective R and a subjective B interference. The next position shows the task of introducing no less than five Black Interferences on the same square.

No. 59 BLACK INTERFERENCE ON ONE SQUARE

P. F. Blake, Western Daily Mercury, 1906

Mate in 2

Key Q—K2   Threat Q×P

Black	White
I	2
R—K6	B—Q7
B—K6	Q×QB
K Kt—K6	Kt—KB4
Q Kt—K6	Q×B
P—K6	Q—Q3

A special sub-theme is the Grimshaw, in which two Black pieces interfere with each other in turn, shown in No. 58, where R – K3 interferes with the B, and B – K3 with the R, and in No. 59 by the moves R – K6 and B – K6. The Grimshaw Theme may be doubled in two ways: (a) by using two distinct pairs of pieces (b) by making a single pair mutually interfere with each other in four ways. The first of these occurs in No. 60, in which the curious appearance of the four units on one line obtained the apt nick-name "Organ-Pipes" from its first inventor, Sam Loyd, in 1857.

No. 60 DOUBLE R AND B GRIMSHAW
A. P. Powell. Empire Review, Sept. 1924

Mate in 2

Key Q—Q4

Black	White
1	2
B—Kt2	Q—Q7
R—Kt2	Q—Q5
B—Kt3	Q—Q6
R—Kt3	Kt—Q8

When the pairs of mutually interfering pieces are sep-arated, F. Janet calls them "Split Organ-Pipes." The second way of doubling the Grimshaw occurs in No. 61.

No. 61 DOUBLE R AND B. GRIMSHAW
J. Hartong. Good Companion Folder, March 1919

Mate in 2

Key B × P

Threats Q—K5 or R—B6

Black	White
1	2
R—Q5	Kt—K3
B—Q5	B—Kt1
R—Q3	Kt—K7
B—Q3	Q—QB2

Here, all the interference play lies between the Black KR and B, and it should be particularly noted that a fifth interference between these pieces occurs by 1. B – K2, allowing 2. Q – R7. If only 1. R – K2 could be made an interference, we should have a Triple R and B Grimshaw.

Every kind of Black unit can interfere with another objectively, and all, except the Kt, can be interfered with. The K can commit a very determined form of suicide, by getting in the way of a defensive piece, and the Self-Block Theme has shown how his powers can be curtailed subjectively.

Subjective Interference of the Black Q is a popular idea, with all kinds of fascinating sub-themes, such as the fourfold interference of Her Majesty by a single Black Kt. She can, however, only interfere with her own forces when moving on a pinned line.

No. 62   OBJECTIVE BLACK Q INTERFERENCE
G. Guidelli. Good Companion Folder, Dec. 1915

Mate in 2

Key Q—Q4

Threat Q—B6

Black	White
1	2
Q—QB4	R × B
Q—K4	Kt × B
Q—KB4	Q—Kt7

The pinned Q interferes with each R and her B in turn in this fine composition. It appears impossible that four interferences by the Q can ever be attained.

The Q can be a party to Mutual Interference, but with rather barren results, and, it appears, with the necessity of a rather brutal threat. An example of a Q and R Grimshaw appears in the next problem, each piece, in turn, on interfering with the other, being pinned in the mate. Incidentally, this is a Black Anti-Bristol, the two pieces masking each other's powers by moving over the critical squares, Black's K2 and K4.

No. 63 Q AND R GRIMSHAW
(BLACK ANTI-BRISTOL)
E. Palkoska. Schachwelt, June 1912

Mate in 2

Key Q—R6. Threats Kt—K5 or 7
If 1. Q—K3, 2. Kt—K5, and if 1. R—K3, 2. Kt—K7.

This sort of thing is the nearest approach that the Two-Mover can show to the Plachutta Theme, or interference between Black pieces of the *same* motion.

Objective and Subjective Interferences of R and B have appeared sufficiently in previous positions, where also Objective Interference by the Kt and P is to be seen. Subjective Interference of a P is, of course, only possible on the sixth rank, preventing it from making its double jump, as in No. 64 by 1. B – K3, which, combined with 1. P – K3, interfering with the same B, makes a Grimshaw Theme.

No. 64 SUBJECTIVE INTERFERENCE OF P
(B AND P GRIMSHAW)
B. Harley. Reading Observer, May 1913

Mate in 2

Key Q—K4

Threat Q × KP

If 1. B—K3, 2. Q × KB
If 1. P—K3 2. Q—R7

In another variation, 1. P – K4 interferes with the KB, but this B cannot be made to interfere with the P. The Double "Pawn" Grimshaw, as it may be called for short (the R and B Grimshaw is also shortened to the "Rook" Grimshaw) is an impossibility. Here follows an unique achievement, three pairs of Grimshaws.

No. 65 DOUBLE R GRIMSHAW + P GRIMSHAW
W. and S. Pimenoff. British Chess Federation, 1930

Mate in 2

Key P=Q Threat Q—Q5

Black	White
1	2
R—Kt5	Q × BP
B—Kt5	Q—B4
R—B6	Kt—K2
B—B6	B—K3
B—K3	Q—Kt7
P—K3	Q(Kt8)—Q8

A poor Key, greatly increasing White's strength, but what a task !

A chapter could easily be written on the subjective or objective powers of each Black piece, including all kinds of fancy tasks, but my space permits of only one more example, the Magee Theme, in which four interferences are caused by two Black P's. (Three such interferences comprise the "Magee Junior" Theme.)

No. 66 MAGEE THEME
A. C. White. Good Companion Folder. Feb. 1919

Mate in 2

Key R—Kt8   Threat R × Kt

Black	White
1	2
P—B3 ch	Kt—Q6
P—B4 ch	Kt—B4
P—Q3	Q × B
P—Q4	Kt × Kt

J. F. Magee founded (in Philadelphia, 1913) the Good Companion Chess Club, which became a problem organization of six hundred members. He is not a composer, and the above theme was a complimentary dedication to him.

In every case of Black Interference so far shown, White has been allowed to mate by reason of Black's cutting off self-control of a mating square, or a square of interposal on the mating line. There is, however, the possibility of the Black Interference *unpinning* a White unit, which proceeds to give mate. This comes quite legitimately under the category of a Self-Interference variation, though it is dignified by the hyphenated name of "Interference-Unpin" and will be exemplified in the next section, devoted to Black Unpins.

Black can unpin White in two ways; by withdrawal of the pinning piece (Withdrawal Unpin) or by self-interference on the pin line (Interference Unpin). The first of these was shown as a task in Nos. 19 and 20. More important is the second method, of which No. 21 was an example. Modern composers have done much intensified work in this direction, especially with regard to the White Q. The record of five unpins of this piece, introducing distinct mates, has stood for several years, and one begins to doubt if it can be surpassed, although the fact that the task can be done with a flight-square, as in No. 67, was once considered a hopeful sign.

No. 67 FIVEFOLD UNPIN OF WHITE Q BY INTERFERENCE

J. E. Funk. Good Companion Folder, Dec. 1920

Mate in 2

Key P—K7 Threat P=Q

Black	White
1	2
QR—B6	Q×RP
KR—QB6	Q×KtP
Kt—K4	Q—Q5
Kt—B3	Q—B4
P—B3	Q—Q7

A remarkable achievement. The Q is here pinned diagonally. A lateral Pin of the lady has been made to yield the same maximum of five Unpins.

The Unpin of every White piece (obviously excepting the

K), both laterally and diagonally, has been much studied. I cannot resist giving a curious double Kt Unpin by the famous young Italian, whose death was such a loss to the Problem world.

No. 68 UNPIN OF WHITE KT BY INTERFERENCE

G. Guidelli. Good Companion Folder, Feb. 1916

Mate in 2

Key Kt—B7 Threat Q—B3

Black	White
1	2
KtP=Kt	Kt—K3
QP=Kt	Kt—Q2

A rare task is the *general* unpinning of White force by moves of a particular Black piece, and as far as I know, only unpin by the Black K has been so treated, yielding three Unpins on two lines, as the maximum.

The last kind of thematised Black mistake, to be shown in this chapter, is the Self-Pin. There are three methods:
(a) K move to the pin line.
(b) Capture on the line.
(c) Departure from the line, thus leaving another unit pinned.

(a) is shown in No. 69.

73

No. 69 BLACK SELF-PIN BY K MOVE

Ella M. Harley. Observer, Feb. 1923

Mate in 2

Key B—R5

Black	White
1	2
K × R (B3)	B—B3
K × R (B5)	Q—Kt3
K—K5	Q—K5

Three nice variations in a waiting position, and an excellent Key. The reader will understand that the essence of the theme lies in the prevention of defence to the mate *by means of the Pin*—in short, a "Pin-Mate" should result.

Another way of piling up the device is to cause several Black units to be pinned by a single K move, the idea being repeated in one variation. This can easily be overdone, and I have noticed that beginners are often attracted by it.

(b) I am not aware that much has been done to thematise Black Self-Pin by capture; as A. C. White remarks, such moves frequently accompany the Cross-check Theme and are rarely worked for by themselves. No. 70 is a fair example.

No. 70 BLACK SELF-PIN BY CAPTURE

G. Dobbs. Good Companion Folder, Nov. 1919

Mate in 2

Key B—Kt3   Threat Kt—B4

Black	*White*
1	2
Q×Kt	R—QR7
R×Kt ch	P—B4
R×P	Kt—B6

Mansfield has, quite recently, taken up this theme with as much success as its rather ungracious nature permits.

(c) Lastly, we have Black Self-Pin by removal of one unit off the pin-line, leaving another unit pinned. This theme has been studied more intensively than any other of recent years, in almost all possible combinations of the two critical Black units, and in conjunction with other prominent two-move themes, such as Self-Interference, Pin, Unpin, and Cross-Check play. The "Half-Pin" Theme, so named by a great exponent, Mansfield, was brought to light in 1855, but scarcely touched by composers until the members of the "Good Companion Club" rediscovered it in 1915.

J. L. Millins. Observer, Oct. 1920

Mate in 2

Key B—K3, waiting

Black	White
1	2
KB any, except × B	Q × R
QB any	Q—K5
R or Kt × R	Q × B

In all three variations, Black self-pins a piece by removal of another from the "Half-Pin lines," which lead from the White R on Kt4 to the Black K, and from the White KB to the Black K. It is an essential part of the theme that the piece left on the line would prevent the actual mate, if it were not pinned. We describe the two Black B's as "half-pinned" in the initial position by the White R, and the other pair, the Black R and Kt, by the White B. The first two variations given above display the *complete* Half-Pin: that is to say, distinct Pin-Mates occur after moves by either Black B. On the other hand, only one Pin-Mate follows moves by the second half-pinned pair (Q × B) and this line accordingly yields only the *incomplete* theme.   In this latter form, the Half-Pin idea is not considered to be worth the force employed, and it should be so used, only as a device to control recalcitrant Black force, or to prevent Cooks or Duals.   It must also be pointed out that the incomplete Half-pin Battery in No. 71 is *artificial.*   No variety is added by the presence of the White KB and Black QKt, since moves such as 1. R × R would force 2. Q × B in any case; these additions of "fringe" force (*i.e.,* superfluous to the real theme) merely introduce a sophistical complication into the mate.

The Half-Pin theme can be achieved with any combination of two Black pieces, on a lateral or diagonal line with the Black K, except two diagonal P's, when it is impossible to get a Pin-Mate due to the one beyond the K's field.   The possible "loci," or spots, of the half-pinned units with regard to the Black K, whether crowded next him as in No. 71, or spread out, have been assiduously studied by composers, and it has become quite difficult to find new combinations.   As many as three complete Half-Pin outfits have been combined in one two-mover, no mean task, considering the expensive nature of the theme.

This chapter ends with some consideration of themes based on variations arising from the different Black pieces, without regard to the particular strategy employed.   The next five examples show the powers of the Q, R, B, Kt and P respectively, in producing a large number of variations.   No special comment is necessary, except that the Black Kt, whether complete in its wheel as in No. 75, or incomplete as in No. 43, is the most popular piece to use in this connection, and appears to work in most easily with strategic ideas.   The Pickaninny Theme, as the set of four variations produced by a single Black P is called, is a poor second in this respect. No. 73 shows the seven moves of a R on *one* line.   A. C. White, a great "taskmaster," has produced eleven variations from moves of this piece on *two* lines.   Myself when young achieved the task of No. 73 on identical lines, except in the "fringe" variations by the other Black force.   Years after its publication, I came across Rowland's complete anticipation.

No. 72 BLACK Q VARIATIONS
G. Heathcote. Pittsburg Gazette, Nov. 1912

Mate in 2

Key Kt—B1   Threat Kt × Q

Here the Black Q accounts for 14 variations, the most so far attained.

No. 73 BLACK R VARIATIONS
T. B. Rowland. The Problem Art, 1887

Mate in 2

Key R—Kt6, waiting

Seven variations are caused by moves of the Black R.

No. 74 BLACK B VARIATIONS

A. C. White. Les Tours De Force, 1906

Mate in 2
Key Q—Q3
Threat P × B

Each of the eight moves by the B forces a distinct mate. The record is nine.

No. 75 BLACK KT WHEEL

G. Heathcote. Hampstead Express, 1905

Mate in 2
Key QR—B7
Threat Kt—B3

In this famous problem each move of the Black Kt defeats the threat, and eight different mates are produced, the maximum possible, without a single capture of the Kt.

No. 76 BLACK P VARIATIONS
(PICKANINNY THEME)
F. Janet. Good Companion Folder, Dec. 1914

Mate in 2

Key Q × P Threat Q × KP

Black	White
1	2
P × P	B × KtP
P—B3	KKt—B4
P × Kt	B—Kt2
P—B4	B × P (B3)

No. 77 is an example of seven variations *due* to a Black R, not necessarily following his moves, as will be seen, but all permitted by different curtailments of his activities. It would be easy to give similar examples affecting the other Black pieces, but a single one must suffice here.

No. 77 F. Janet
Victory Tournament, Hastings, 1919

Mate in 2

Key Kt—Kt5

Threat Q × R

Black	White
1	2
R × R ch	P × R
R else on file	Kt × P
Kt—Q3	R—K7
Kt—Q5	Kt—Q6
Kt—K6	Kt—Kt3
B—Q5	P—B7
B—K6	Q × B

CHAPTER VI

MATING STRATEGY

In White's second and final move, the scope for complication is less than in the previous play, but quite enough themes can arise for a chapter. We have the following sections:—

(a) A large number of mates given by the same unit, directly or by discovery.

(b) The special device of mate by different P promotions.

(c) "Avoidance" in mating.

(d) White Interference.

(e) Pin-Mates.

(f) Echo Mates.

(g) Mirror Mates.

(h) Model Mates.

(i) Changed and Added Mates, treated separately in Chapter VIII.

(a) As above, given by direct mates. Taking the most powerful piece first, the maximum of twelve fatal blows by She Who Must Be Obeyed is known as the Queen's Cross Theme. It is of some historical interest, having attracted composers of more than one generation.

No. 78 QUEEN'S CROSS

M. Marble. La Stratégie, Sept. 1907

Mate in 2

Key R—B4.   Threats Q × KR and Q × B

The reader can easily work out the 12 variations himself. Economy of force is a noteworthy feature here. The repetitive mates by capture of the R and QB on the same line (i.e. after 1. R – B4 ch and R – Kt4, and 1. B – K5 and KB6) are called *Herlins*, after an early composer.   Found abundantly in the old-type "Waiter," they are not exciting.

Themes based on multiple direct mates by pieces other than the Q are not of great interest, as a rule; each can give only two mates against a fixed Black K, increased, when he has flights and with the aid of checking keys, to four by a single R or P and five by a B.   Direct mates by the pieces *in pairs* are not much more productive of a good theme, four mates by two White Kt's being the most frequently seen, and they nearly always occur as incidental to really strategic play.   When mates are given by discovery, there is much more scope for the piling up of variations.   The White K can be made to discover six mates, either diagonally or laterally, the R fourteen, the B thirteen, the Kt eight, and the P four (disregarding promotion tasks), all these being maxima; (the Q evidently cannot move, discovering check).

Examples for each piece follow.

No. 79 K DISCOVERIES
C. L. Fitch. Detroit Free Press, April 1879

Mate in 2

Key Q—K3, waiting

The White K goes to each of six squares in turn.

No. 80 R DISCOVERIES
N. Schalit and T. Maendl. Good Companion Folder, May 1921

Mate in 2

Key Q—B1. Threat R any

Here the White R is forced to every possible square by various Black moves.

No. 81 B DISCOVERIES

H. & E. Bettmann. St. John Globe, 1885

Mate in 2

Key R—R4.

Threat B any

As with the White R of No. 80, the B occupies every square within his reach.

No. 82 KT DISCOVERIES
"WHITE KNIGHT TOUR"

A. Bottacchi. Eighth American Chess Congress, 1921

Mate in 2

Key R—Kt4

Threat R—Kt8

The complete White Knight Tour is a very easy task (whereas the Black Knight Wheel, shown in No. 75, is a difficult business) and unless it can be done neatly and with the addition of some other feature (as the Unpin device of No. 82, in which the Black Q forces the entire tour) it had better be left alone.

No. 83 P DISCOVERIES

J. C. J. Wainwright. Wanderer, 1888

Mate in 2

Key B—Q6. Threat P—K3

Black	White
1	2
P×Q	P—K4
R×Q	P×R
P—Q6	P×P

A charming little problem, with much ingenuity displayed in forcing all possible alternatives.

(b) Pawn Promotions.

Chess Editors well know that the knighting of a P, particularly as a Key, has a great fascination for the novice composer, who little realises the antiquity of the device, and sends in his effort with rejoicing heart, just as I did in my own salad days.   I am not dealing with Keys here, but may say in passing that P promotion as a Key of a two-mover is very rare, and generally due to the impossibility of getting

any other to work.   In the mate, only two effective changes
can be rung, the choice between Q and Kt, for clearly a Q
could always be substituted for a R or B.   Notwithstanding
this limitation of the task, some very fine work has been done
in the theme.   In the example below, a single P becomes a
Q and Kt on three squares, yielding six variations.

No. 84 WHITE P PROMOTIONS

H. W. Bettmann. Good Companion Folder, Jan. 1923

Mate in 2

Key R—Q7

Black	*White*
I	2
K × R	P × R (Kt)
K × B	P—B8 (Kt)
R—B1	P × Kt (Kt)
Kt × R	P × R (Q)
Kt—K3	P—B8 (Q)
K—B1	P × Kt (Q)

The maximum task is carried out beautifully and most
economically.   Effects with two or more P's have been also
well studied, and the reader may remember the amusing
No. 18.   Later on he will find No. 147, with its extraordinary
promotion changes.

(c) Avoidance in Mating.

Diagrams 79 to 83 have shown very well how the moving piece in a discovered mate can be forced to different squares, in order to defeat Black's counter-attack. A more subtle device, generally to compel a series of mates from one White Battery, is *Avoidance* by White of Interference with his own force. Such interference may affect either the cover of a flight-square or the Pin of a Black unit, and the theme consists in inducing such Black moves as will make the "Avoidance" harmless.

No. 85 AVOIDANCE IN MATING

C. Mansfield. Hampshire Post, Jan. 1915

Mate in 2

Key R—B2.   Threat B × Q

Black	White
I	2
Q × B, Q—Q6	Kt—Q3 (× Q)
Q—K5	Kt—Kt3

Here, after 1. Q × B, the Kt must go to Q3, avoiding both Kt3, which would unpin the Black B, and K2, which would cut off the cover of QR2 by the White KR. Other Black defences compel each of these avoided moves in turn, i.e. Q—K5, rendering the Unpin of his B useless to Black because of the Self-Interference, and R × P, a Self-Block

87

allowing Kt – K2. This "Avoidance" is a negative device, as it were, to force a series of highly-specialised mates, and it is scattered throughout modern composition: for example, in No. 46, after 1. Kt × R ch, 2. Kt – Kt5 is the mate, avoiding Kt – B4, which would interfere with the guard on K4. A second example of Avoidance in mating, with a waiting Key, is appended.

No. 86 AVOIDANCE IN MATING
E. M. & B. Harley. Observer, March 1926

Mate in 2

Key R—KKt1

Black	White
1	2
B—B2	Kt—B5
P—Q5	Kt—B3
Q—Kt5	Kt—Kt2

Unpins of both the Black Q and KB, and "White Interference" are avoided and permitted in turn, by inducing Black to interfere with the Pin-lines, or to block his K.

For the special avoidance known as the Schiffmann Defence, see No. 167.

(d) *White Self-Interference Mates.*

Mates following Black Self-Blocks have already been dealt

with in Chapter V. This is by far the most frequent method of introducing "White Interference," but two other ways should be mentioned.

(1) The mate opens up a Battery, covering the square which is cut off by the same move. This may seem to be a contradiction in terms, until No. 31 is examined, where the Kt – Q3 threat brings the Q into action against QKt5, and cuts off the same square from the KB's control.

(2) Black opens up a White guard on to the cut-off square. This theme has received much attention of late from the brilliant young Russian School. No 87 shows five examples.

No. 87 WHITE INTERFERENCE BY OPEN GATE

B. J. de C. Andrade and B. Harley. Observer, June 1930

Mate in 2

Key P × P

Black	White
1	2
Q—B2	P—KB4
Q—K5	P × Q
Q × KP, Q—B5	Kt—B4
Q—Kt4	P—K4
KKt any (except × P)	Kt—K7

To make the theme clear, take the first variation. The Black Q opens a gate for, or "lets through" the action of White's QB, which then holds Q4, enabling the reply, P – KB4, to interfere with the White R's control of the critical Q4 square. The capture Key seems to me to be extremely "thematic," in that it "creates a Whiteness" on Q4, the critical square in four of the variations. A *White* unit on this square is unfavourable to the White forces, which must strive to get rid of the disadvantage by inducing the "let throughs," or "Line Evacuations," as T. R. Dawson prefers to call them. The problem (which, by the way, was the first example by either of the composers to contain the full White force) led to a discussion as to the correct definition of a Thematic Key. I maintained that the expression should be confined to such theme-introducing Keys as create critical, or unfavourable, squares or lines for White; or, alternatively, favourable squares or lines for Black. In short, a Thematic Key should be some kind of Gift Key. Andrade wished to use the expression universally for all Keys that definitely introduced the main theme. Look at No. 168. The Key introduces three thematic variations, by the Q's ambush behind the Black Kt. There is no Gift here, but the opposite feature, Provision for Black moves, which is in general an inferior opening. One might, of course, discriminate between good and poor Thematic Keys, but I prefer to use the words in a laudatory sense only.

(e) *Pin-Mates*

The term was defined in connection with No. 69. Such mates, due to Black Self-Pin, were illustrated by this Problem and its two successors. There remains the case where the White mate itself introduces the Pin. In No. 88, mate is given by discovery, the moving piece pinning each of two Black pieces. Pin-Mates by White operation are not of themselves a very fruitful field and two examples will suffice. In the Guidelli the effect is deliberately worked for; in the Mansfield, No. 89, it is more or less an incident in the variation play.

No. 88 PIN-MATES BY WHITE ACTION
G. Guidelli. Good Companion Folder, Nov. 1918

Mate in 2

Key R—Kt4, waiting

Black	White
1	2
R—B8	Kt × R
P=Q	Kt × P

The White Q and QKt here form a "Masked" Battery, the Black P masking their operation against the K in the diagram, and unmasking it in the second variation.

No. 89 PIN-MATES BY WHITE ACTION
C. Mansfield. Argentine Tourney, 1926

Mate in 2

Key Q—K7

Threat R × Kt

If 1. Kt × P, 2. R – B4.   In this masterpiece on the Half-Pin theme, the two Pin-Mates due to White action are only a small part of the Half-Pin scheme, which yields no less than six thematic mates, five given by moves of the White

QR. The second variation, 1. Kt × P, involves a *double* Pin-Mate, due to both Black's move and White's reply.

On the subject of Double Pin-Mates, I must quote a pretty affair containing two examples, by a lady who specialises in this particular way of killing the Black K. The excellent Key adds two flight-squares to the one set in the diagram.

No. 90 DOUBLE PIN-MATES

Ella M. Harley. Empire Review, Dec. 1925

Mate in 2

Key R—QR6. Threat Q—B6

Black	White
1	2
K × R (R3)	Q—B6
K × R (R5)	Kt × R

In each variation the same Black R and B are thematically pinned.

(f) *Echo Mates*

A. C. White defines the word "Echo" in a very wide sense, as the repetition of any particular element in a problem, so that practically all "Tasks" would come under this heading. I have, however, more often heard it in a restricted sense, indicating *positional* imitation of one variation by another;

symmetrical mates, with regard to the Black K, for instance, as in the two variations given in No. 88, and other ordinary uses of a White Kt to give two mates; or, where Black moves are in question, manoeuvres like the mutual interference between the R's and B's in No. 60, or the Star-Flight Theme (No. 17). In the Chameleon Echo, the Black K is mated symmetrically on White and Black squares.

No. 91 CHAMELEON ECHO MATE

H. von Gottschall. Bohemia, Oct. 1907

Mate in 2

Key Q—KR7. Threat Q—B5

If 1. K – B3, 2. Q – K7. In these two mates, the positions of the White Q and both Kt's, relatively to the Black K, are identical.

(g) In a *Mirror Mate*, the Mated Black K must have no unit of either colour on any contiguous square—he must see his reflection all round him. There is practically no strategic consideration involved in the mirror, which is a purely fanciful idea, not well adapted to thematic rendering in the two-mover. There *is* a problem extant in which the lone-lorn K is mated in fourteen ways, but it is hardly worth quoting. From the "picture" point of view, a Mirror Mate is pretty

93

enough, and the effect is heightened when the mate is both "pure" and "economical," terms that are defined as follows:
(h) *Model Mates.*

Two preliminary definitions must be understood.

(1) A Pure mate is a mate in which every square next the Black K is guarded once only.

(2) An Economical mate is one in which all the *White* force (with the allowable exception of K and P's) is employed in some way or other.

A. A PURE, BUT UNECONOMICAL MATE

Taking the squares next the Black K, notice that four squares are guarded only by the White R, namely QB6, Q6, K5 and K4; two by the White KB, QB4 and K6, and two by the QB, QB5 and Q4. In no case is there a double guard on any of the eight squares. This accordingly is a *Pure* mate. Note that *the square on which the Black K is placed* may be doubly guarded without effecting the purity of the position; that is to say, a double check may give a Pure mate. Some composers hold that the K's square is impure, if the *doubling* of the check is not a necessity in the mate.

Considering next the White force in Diagram A, we see that three units are used to give the mate, the R and both B's; the White K, Kt and P's are merely spectators.   By the definition of an Economical mate, the question is not affected by the employment or non-employment of K and P's; the White Kt, and this unit alone, makes the mate uneconomical. (For "Bohemian" Economy, see my remarks after Diagram C.)

B. AN ECONOMICAL, BUT IMPURE MATE

Moving five pieces in diagram A one square in a N.W. direction, we arrive at an Economical mate, the White Kt now being necessary to guard Q4 square. It must be emphasized that *White* force only affects the question of economy; any number of Black pieces put into diagram B would not invalidate this factor.

The mate shown above is, however, no longer pure—for three reasons:

(1) K5 is held by both the R and White QB.

(2) K6 is held by a B and P, and

(3) K4 is held by the R and blocked by the Black B.

Each of these double covers of squares is sufficient by itself to spoil the purity of the mate.

By simply removing the Kt from Diagram A, we get a mate that is both pure and economical, and therefore a "Model" (a term invented by H. D'O. Bernard) and a very familiar specimen, I may add. Three more well-worn

Models, showing some of the possibilities of the White Q and Kt's, appear on one diagram, C, to save space. That on the lower right-hand part of the board is called a *Sideboard Model*, with reference to the position of the Black K. It has been suggested that such mates should not rank as Models, if there were double cover of any square next the Black K on an imaginary board joined to the real one. In the example, the square on his right hand, covered, according to this over-subtle argument, by the White Q and Kt, would be impure, a contention that has not found general favour.

C. THREE FAMILIAR MODEL MATES
BY Q AND KT'S

The other two mates in Diagram C exemplify special kinds of Models. That on the left is, as the reader will recognise, a Mirror Mate, and the combination is called a *Mirror-Model*. Highly attractive as these "pictures" are, there remains very little to be done with them, the few combinations possible in one problem having been thoroughly exploited. The position on the top right-hand is a *Primary Model*, *all* the White force being employed. Here again, the severe restrictions imposed by the usual Model feature are so heightened that originality is almost impracticable; (the rarest of all mates, a Primary Mirror-Model, has been called a Prime Mate).

The strict Bohemian School insists that all White P's present in the diagram shall be employed in a Model Mate, while the use of the White K remains optional. Great artists as many of them are, the Bohemians, in Western eyes, sometimes let their passion for Picture Mates carry them too far. All other considerations often appear to be quite secondary, and Keys that deprive the Black K of one or more flights, without any strategic compensation, are by no means rare.

Coming to the application of the theme in the Two-Mover, the Model-Mate is rarely found in modern work. This is due both to the exhaustion of possible combinations, already mentioned, and the difficulty of introducing it into strategic variations; in the Three-Mover and longer problems, it is quite another story. The device that yields Models most easily in the Two-Mover is sacrifice.

No. 92 MODELS BY SACRIFICE
M. Havel. Illustrovany Svet, Dec. 1903

Mate in 2

Key R—B6. Threat B—B3

Black	White
1	**2**
K×R	Q—K7
B×R	Q—K4
B×B	B—B3

The first of these mates, delivered by the Q with her two B's assistance, is a hoary chestnut, and the same may be said of the third, which in essence is a Model by a B, assisted by R and another B. This last mate is the threat, and becomes a Model only by Black's obliging aid in capturing the KB. Such Models, following non-defensive moves, are, of course, extremely artificial, and are called "Slaughter" Models. The Bohemian Two-Mover largely exploits this kind of mate.

In the next example we have no less than four Primary Models, which must, I think, be the record number in a Two-Move Problem. Those following 1. either Kt × Kt are further instances of "Slaughter."

No. 93 PRIMARY MODELS

H. L. Schuld. Tidskrift, Nov. 1904

Mate in 2

Key Kt—B2. Threat Kt × QKt

Black	White
1	2
QKt × Kt	Q—QKt7
KKt × Kt	Q—R1
Kt—B3	P—K4

In all four mates, the total White force, including K and P's, has a definite use in guarding the Black K's field. A fifth Model, not a Primary one, follows 1. K – B3, when two White P's take no part in the mate, Kt × Q Kt. This gives me the occasion of pointing out that exactly the same disposition of White force is allowed to give distinct Models, when the mated Black K occupies different squares, as here, but the lack of contrast, as compared with different White arrangements, produces an effect of dullness.

Concurrent Models occur, when a White piece gives mate on different squares of the same line with the Black K and on the same side of him, the other White force being unchanged. If, in No. 93, the Q mated on QR8 as well as QKt7, following different Black defences, we should call these distinct but Concurrent Models. The actual mates, Q – QKt7 and R1, are *not* Concurrent, her Majesty delivering the blow on different sides of the K. This feature of Concurrency, by the way, applies to ordinary (non-model) mates, when there is no real difference in the strategy. The Herlins of No. 78 show my meaning.

A full list of the features that are generally considered to constitute distinction in Model Mates now follows:

(1) When the Black K is mated on different squares.

(2) When the same mating piece is on different squares.

(3) When mate is given by different pieces.

(4) When there is a change in the guard of the Black K's field, either in the White or Black force so used.

These four rules were propounded by the late A. F. Mackenzie in "Chess Lyrics" some twenty-five years ago, and found, I believe, almost universal acceptance. They simply amount to saying that any difference, however slight, in the critical force, constitutes distinction of Model Mates.

No. 94, with its startling Key and four unexpected Models, shows what a master-hand can accomplish with a small White force.

No. 94 MODELS WITH FLIGHTS AND P PROMOTIONS

E. Palkoska. Tidskrift, Sept. 1907

Mate in 2

Key Q—Kt5

Threat KP = Q

Black	White
1	2
P × Q	KP=Q
K × KP	Q—K8
K × BP	P=Q
K—K4	Q—K2

No. 95 shows the record number of non-concurrent Models achieved in a Two-Mover. It is the neatest of several similar positions, but the Key is a drastic one.

No. 95 SIX MODELS, WITHOUT CONCURRENCY

J. Keeble. Leeds Mercury, 1901

Mate in 2

Key B—Q6

Black	White
1	2
QKt any	Kt—K7
KKt any	Kt—B7
RP × P	Kt—K3
KtP × P	Kt—B3
B × QKt	P—K4
B × KKt	P—B4

The last four mates are Slaughter Models, and all six, taken in pairs, usefully illustrate the Echo Model feature.

I now come to a special Art-Mate known as the Pin-Model. Of comparatively recent growth, it has added a slight lease of life to the Bohemian Two-Mover, but its best expression, from considerations of novelty and strategy, is to be found, as with its humble brother, the ordinary Model, in longer problems. The Pin-Model is a Model Pin-Mate, for which the rules of purity and economy are specially made elastic. The pinning White Unit, in that it is necessary for the mate, is deemed economical, and should the pinned Black unit stand next to his K, his square is allowed to be pure, although it follows, as a matter of course, that it is doubly held. This square, however, must not be controlled in a third manner, and in all other respects the usual rules apply. An example follows, containing three non-concurrent Pin-Models, the record attained, I believe, in a Two-Mover.

No. 96 THREE PIN-MODELS
J. Volf. Lidove Noviny, 1905

Mate in 2

Key Kt—B3

Threat Q—R4

Black	White
1	2
R×R	Q—R7
Q×R	Q—QKt1
R×P	Kt×P

Both Black R's and the Q are crucially pinned, in turn; in the first two cases the pinned pieces are in the Black K's field, when Q5 is pure, notwithstanding its cover by the White KB, a piece that is economical, since it prevents intervention by the pinned piece. In the third variation, no question of purity arises, and the White Q becomes economical, preventing 2. R × Kt. It is of interest to note that 1. R × Kt yields a plain Model by 2. P × R.

CHAPTER VII

COMBINATION THEMES

This chapter illustrates, in a rather haphazard way, some of the complex schemes that have been so largely developed in the last few years. Many hundreds, if not thousands, of diagrams would be required to cover the whole ground, of which only a small selection can be made here. For the rest, students are referred to "The Good Companion Two-Mover" by G. Hume and A. C. White; and even that monumental work could be much expanded. George Hume, the Nottingham veteran, who now has charge of the A. C. White Problem Collection, has collaborated with A. C. W. in the production of his Christmas books for some fifteen years, testing, verifying, and supervising these standard problem works at every stage. His colleague has called him "The Presiding Destiny of the Series." A book of Hume's own compositions, "Changing Fashions," appeared in 1925. The latest of the series by these two great connoisseurs has just reached me. It is entitled "Valves and Bi-Valves," and deals with the theme of No. 117 in this chapter, and some allied effects.

In the following examples complex *variations* are mainly studied, and not the occurrence, side by side in a problem, of different types of strategy.

As the *Half-Pin Theme* lends itself, at least as well as any other, to combination with other ideas, I will begin with some of its possibilities. First, with the Cross-Check Theme, we have No. 97.

C. G. Watney. Good Companion Folder, Feb. 1922
(Developed from a version by C. Promislo).

Mate in 2

Key Kt×P. Threat Q—B8

Black	White
1	2
Kt×Kt ch	R—Q4
Kt else ch ⎱ Q—Q5 ch ⎰	Kt—B4
Q×Kt ch	Kt—B5

As usual, I give only those variations that exemplify the main theme.

Note the splendour of the Key, which allows the Black R and Kt Battery to open against the White K, and gives the Black Q a couple of checks; it is also a threefold sacrifice of the Kt, and all that can be said against it is the capture of an immovable P. Taking the variations in order, the first, Kt×Kt ch 2. R–Q4, besides fulfilling the theme-combination, self-pins the Kt, which could otherwise interpose on B5. In the second variation, the key piece switchbacks, an amusing feature, following, in the first case, Self-Pin of the Black Q (note also the avoidance of 2. Kt – K4, which would unpin that piece) and in the second case, Self-Pin of the Black Kt; really distinct variations in essence, though the mating move is the same. The third variation, Q × Kt ch, 2. Kt – B5, besides the theme, contains, as in the first, Self-Pin of the *moving* piece. Following a system that I evolved (published in a "Good Companion" Folder) of giving relative marks to problems for complexity, this position scores the highest number of any that I have come across.

No. 98 combines the Half-Pin with both Black and White Self-Interference.

No. 98 HALF-PIN + INTERFERENCE

G. C. Alvey. Observer, Sept. 1920

Mate in 2

Key Q—Kt2. Threat R—B5

Black	White
1	2
B—Q4 ch	R—B4
B—Q5	Kt—Q3
Kt—Q4	Kt—B6

In the first two variations, the Black R is cut off by his B's, and in the third, the White Kt is enabled to interfere with his own B. The embellishments of a Cross-Check and an ordinary Self-Block accompany the Black B defences.

In first-class complex problems, it is usual to find such little grace notes added to the theme, partly, of course, because the composer works for them, but also arising from the necessity of the case; for instance, if 1. B – Q4 were *not* check, the "star" mate 2. R – B4 would be hopelessly dualised by QR × B (forced, it may be added, by 1. B × KBP), and without the Black K's flight, which must be blocked by 1. B – Q5, the whole scheme would doubtless fall to the ground. I believe this problem to be the best example of the doubling of the Half-Pin theme. Its much-lamented composer has interwoven the thematic pieces of the two lines in a beautiful way. It will be well worth the reader's while to examine the whole play, and discover how the sets of half-pinned units interact on each other. The three variations shown above are examples, and I will mention also 1. R – Q5, which blocks the flight, upsets the White Battery, and allows the thematic Pin-Mate, P = Q.

No. 99 contains four distinct Self-Blocks, in conjunction with Half-Pinning.

No. 99 HALF-PIN + SELF-BLOCKS

A. Bottacchi. Italia Scacchistica, May 1918

Mate in 2

Key Kt—K6

Threat Q—K4

Black	White
1	2
R × Kt	Q—Kt5
R—B5	Q × P
Kt—B4	Kt (K6)—B7
Kt—Q3	Kt (K8)—B7

Self-blocking being a comparatively simple idea, involving one unit only, the Italian composer was able to get a nice, open rendering, in contrast to most Half-Pin combination themes.

The unpinning of a single White unit by the move of a half-pinned Black piece was studied by Guidelli in 1916; but some five years passed before Hume doubled the stratagem, naming the theme shown in the next diagram.

No. 100 DOUBLE HALF-PIN + UNPIN OF WHITE (HUME THEME)

A. Ellerman. Good Companion Folder, March 1922

Mate in 2

Key Q × P. Threat R × B

If 1. Kt – B6, 2. Q – K4. If 1. Kt – Q6, 2. P – K4. If 1. Q – Q6, 2. Q – B7. Each of the two half-pinned pieces performs the Unpinning operation, and yields a thematic Pin-Mate. The Black Kt does it twice, first interfering with his companion in the Half-Pin, and next with an outside piece, the QB. Hume and White, in "The Good Companion Two-Mover," distinguish these manoeuvres as *Internal* and *External* Interference of the pins, while 1. Q – Q6 represents the comparatively simple *Withdrawal* Unpin.

In the *Inverted Hume Theme*, the two half-pinned units

pin, instead of unpinning White, who is able to deliver the thematic Pin-Mates, in consequence of these defences.

No. 101 DOUBLE HALF-PIN + PIN OF WHITE (INVERTED HUME THEME)

K. S. Howard. Observer, Dec. 1926

Mate in 2

Key Q—Q4. Threat Q × P (Kt 2)

If 1. Kt – B5, 2. Q – B3 (White QKt is pinned). If 1. P – Kt6, 2. Kt – Kt5 (Q is pinned). The second variation also shows the Dalton Theme, where a Black unit (here the P on Kt5) unpinned by the Key, in turn pins the Key piece, defeating the threat by its move. The old nursery jargon comes to mind, as one studies these intricate packets of pins: "The stick began to beat the dog, the dog began to bite the pig . . ." Weenink, in The Chess Problem, gives a whole chapter on the subject, with an exhaustive classification under ten headings, as follows: 1. *The crucial piece is Black.* (a) White unpins Black (b) Black unpins Black (c) White pins Black (d) Black pins Black (e) Prevention of pin or unpin 2. *The crucial piece is White.* (a) White unpins White (b) Black unpins White (c) White pins White (d) Black pins White (e) Prevention of pin or unpin.

K. A. K. Larsen. Good Companion Folder, Feb. 1920

Mate in 2

Key K—B5. Threat Q—B4

Black	White
1	2
Kt—K4 ch	Kt—QB3

Strictly speaking, the Tuxen Theme (named after a Danish composer) implies Half-Pin combined with Cross-Check and *any* kind of Unpin; *Interference* Unpin is an added point of strategy, which probably carries variation complexity in the two-mover as far as possible, the whole device requiring at least nine units of force. Only one variation displays the whole bag of tricks, though there is other good half-pinning play in 1. QKt else ch and P – Q6 ch. It appears extremely unlikely that the full double theme, exhibited by each of two half-pinned pieces, will ever be achieved.

Before leaving the Half-Pin, I give a position in which the number of flights must, I think, be a record. The addition of this feature hardly constitutes a true strategic combination, but it is worth study as a special task.

No. 103 HALF-PIN + 4 FLIGHTS

C. G. Watney. Good Companion Folder, March 1921

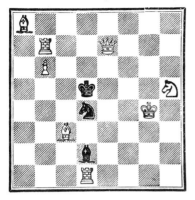

Mate in 2

Key Q—Kt4

Black	White
1	2
Kt—B3	Kt—B4
B any	R—K7

A few *Cross-Check* Theme-combinations are next given. This stratagem has been shown in conjunction with the Half-Pin (No. 97) and Unpin of White (No. 102). Only one case of Unpin occurs in the latter example and the doubling of the theme (the maximum attained so far, I believe) appears below.

No. 104 CROSS-CHECK + UNPINS

A. Ellerman. Observer, July 1920

Mate in 2

Key Kt—B3

Threat Q—Kt4

Black	White
1	2
Q—R2 ch	Kt—Q7
Q×B ch	Kt—Kt4

109

The Half-Pin theme also enters, but the Cross-Check +
Unpin combination is the important feature.

Cross-Check, combined with Unpin of both Black and
White, is shown below. It is called the Larsen Theme.

No. 105 LARSEN THEME

K. A. L. Kubbel. Die Schwalbe, 1929

Mate in 2

Key K—Kt5.   Threat Q × R

If 1. P—B5 ch,   2. Kt—B5

The checking Black defence unpins his QB and the White
KKt. A fine piece of complexity, but, naturally, expensive
in material. I would like to see an example in which the
mate was not a *double* check.

Cross-Checking with Black Interference is a very attractive
device, often met with. No. 24 was a very neat rendering,
with the Grimshaw Mutual Interference of Black R and B,
and I shall give only one more, in which the pinned Black Q
is the protagonist. The Lady must, of course, be pinned in
the mate, whenever she causes line-obstruction of her own
side. No. 106 is one of my War problems, composed at a
village called Dainville, in France, during the last great
German attack.

No. 106 CROSS-CHECK + BLACK Q INTERFERENCE

B. Harley. Western Daily Mercury, Nov. 1918

Mate in 2

Key R—QB3
Threat P—Kt4

Black	White
1	2
Q—Q4 ch	B—Q3
Q—Kt 4 ch	P—B4

The checking Q interferes with her B and KR in turn. I have done this theme with a flight-square (Black's Q5) but it does not come out very neatly, as might be expected.

The next quotation is an expression of Cross-Check with flight squares, both outlets being given by the Key.

No. 107 CROSS-CHECK + FLIGHTS

C. G. Watney. Kent C.A. Tourney, 1920

Mate in 2

Key R—Q3.
Threat R—K7

Black	White
1	2
K—K3 ch	R (Q7)—Q5
K—K5 ch	R (Q3)—Q5

In passing, one may mention two other fine variations, 1.
K – B4, 2. R – K7 (the threat) and 1. Kt – B5, 2. R – K3,
the last a White Interference.

In the next example, Cross-Checks are combined with 3
Self-Blocks, the most so far attained. (Heathcote has also
done the task.)

No. 108 CROSS-CHECK + SELF-BLOCKS
W. Langstaff. Observer, July 1925

Mate in 2

Key Kt—B6.   Threat Kt—B5

Black	White
1	2
R—Q6 ch	KKt—Q4
R—K6 ch	R—B6
R—B6 ch	R—K5

Unpinning with Half-Pinning and Cross-Checking has been
shown. Now follows a specimen of Unpin by Black Interference, in which all four thematic mates are given by White
Kt's, not a strategic principle in itself and therefore not
really a Combined-Theme variation, but of great interest as
a " task."

No. 109 FOUR UNPINS OF WHITE KT'S

T. M. Stott. Observer, Oct. 1921

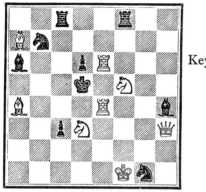

Mate in 2

Key B—Q7. Threat R—Q4

Black	White
1	2
R—B5	Kt—B4
Kt—K7	Kt—Kt4
Kt—B6 ⎱ B—B3 ⎰	Kt—K3
B—B7	Kt—K7

In No. 110 the White Q is unpinned four times by Black P moves, with different mates resulting.

No. 110 FOUR UNPINS OF A Q BY BLACK P'S

J. K. Heydon. Good Companion Folder, Nov. 1920

Mate in 2

Key P—B4, waiting.

Black	White
1	2
P—B6	Q×KP
KP×P *e.p.*	Q—K6
KtP×P *e.p.*	Q—Kt 5
P—Kt6	Q—Q2

An extreme task rendered possible by the "fancy" *en passant* P capture; the flight-taking Key is an unfortunate necessity.

In No. 111, four kinds of pinning and unpinning occur
thematically in one variation.

No. 111 WHITE AND BLACK PIN AND UNPIN

B. Harley. Good Companion Folder, Summer 1919

Mate in 2

Key B—Q2.   Threat Kt—Q6

Black	White
1	2
B—K3	Q × Q

The defence given above unpins the Black Q, which now
prevents the threat, pins the White P (B2) which otherwise
would mate, and unpins the White Q, which is enabled to
mate, the Black KB being self-pinned. This may be called
a "One Variation" Problem, and is, of course, only of value
as a task achievement.

In the next example, a blend of Unpins is shown. The
original version was unfortunately cooked, to the sorrow of
a good many too-confident solvers in my "Observer" chess
column competitions. It was only quite recently that I obtained a revision from the composer, who has otherwise
improved the play in this record task.

C. R. B. Sumner. Observer, Dec. 1924
(A revised version)

Mate in 2

Key Kt—B8. Threat Kt—K6

Black	White
1	2
QKt—K4	Q—Kt 5
KKt—K4	Q × KtP
P—K4	Q × Kt

These three defences unpin both the Black R and White Q simultaneously. A neat additional line is 1. Kt – Kt4 (the only defence to the try 1. Kt – B5) introducing a White Interference, 2. Kt – Kt6.

Only in the last few years have mates introduced by Withdrawal Unpin been systematically studied as "Combination-Variations." The South American, Ellerman, and a group of modern Italian composers have shown great possibilities in the way of Self-Blocks, Black Interferences, Black Self-Pins and Unpins, and Half Pins, more or less denied to the Unpin of White by Interference, in which Black moves are restricted to the pin-line. Two examples follow.

No. 113 WITHDRAWAL UNPIN + BLACK INTERFERENCE

G. Cristoffanini. Pittsburg Post, 1925

Mate in 2

Key B—R6. Threat P × R

Black	White
1	2
R—Kt5	Q—B7
KR—QB5	Q—K6
R—K5	Q—B5

In each case mate by the White Q follows her unpin by one Black unit which interferes with another. In the Unpin by Interference, it is, of course, the *pinning* piece whose powers are interfered with.

No. 114 DIRECT UNPIN OF A BATTERY

A. Mari. Bristol Times, June 1927

Mate in 2

Key P—Q4.
Threat R—K5

Black	White
1	2
Q×P ch	R—Q3
Q×QR	R—B5
Q—Kt4	R—Kt3
Q—B5 or Kt6	R×Q

The unpinned White R goes to four squares. The variations are not of the "combination" kind, as in No. 113.

116

Black and White Interferences can form the main stock
of strategy in a two-mover.   Usually they occur side by side
in separate variations, as below.

No. 115   BLACK   AND   WHITE   INTERFERENCE

B. Harley. Hampshire Post, July 1914

Mate in 2

Key Kt—Kt4.   Threat Kt—Q2

Black	White	Black	White
1	2	1	2
R—B6, Q5	R—K5	P—K4	Kt—B6
R—B7	Q—Q3	Kt—B4	Kt—Kt5
B—B6	Q×B	Kt—K6	Kt—B2

The first four variations illustrate Black, and the last two,
White Interference.   The Key, unmasking the White KR to
cover Q5, cut off by the threat, goes well with the scheme.
Highly interesting is the junction in one variation of both
kinds   of   Interference,   making   a   true   " Combination-
Variation," shown in the next position, which I suggested
to its composer should be called the "Kubla Khan" problem.
Andrade seems to have produced it, and despatched it to its
destination, in a sort of trance.   He had completely forgotten
it, when I mentioned the theme the other day.

No. 116 BLACK AND WHITE INTERFERENCE COMBINED

B. J. de C. Andrade. Newcastle Weekly Chronicle, 1924

Mate in 2

Key Q—B6.
Threat Q × QB

Black	White
1	2
P—K5	Kt—B4
KKt—Q5	B—K4
QKt—Q5	P—K4

In each case Black permits mate not only by interfering with his R, but also by self-blocking, allowing White Interference.

An entertaining theme-combination is the "Valve," where Black simultaneously opens and shuts, by unmasking and interference, his control lines.

No. 117 FOURFOLD VALVE

J. E. Funk. Pittsburg Post, April 1923

Mate in 2

Key Kt—Kt7.
Threat Kt—K8

Black	White
1	2
Kt—QR3	Q × B
Kt—KR3	Kt × P
P—Q3	Q—K6
P—Q4	Q—KB1

In the first two variations, the Black R's are unmasked upon the threat square, while their control of their files is shut off; in the last two, the Black Q's lines are opened and closed. In the Bi-Valve Theme, much more common and easier to construct, a Black move opens up the control line of one piece, and masks the line of another, in contrast to No. 117, where the same piece is affected in both ways. No. 43 gives a Bi-Valve variation in 1. Kt – B3 2. R × B. The Kt opens up control of his R upon the threat square, and masks control of his Q upon his B. In the variation 1. Kt – Q2 2. B – Kt7, the same Black R is affected throughout, and this is therefore a true Valve.

The five themes that have been shown in conjunction with each other, the Cross-Check, Pin, Unpin, Half-Pin and Self-Interference (in which Self-Block may be included), are without doubt the most strategic of all, and I do not consider it necessary to go into combinations of more elementary devices. The reader may have noticed that in nearly every problem so far quoted in this chapter it is the complex variation, in itself, that has been exemplified. Quite distinct from this, is the attempt at joining together in one problem separate strategic features, as in No. 43, which adds Unpin of the White Q to a Black Kt Wheel. In such cases, although there is not unity of idea, there should be considerable unity of force; the pieces taking part in one feature should, as far as possible, be used to carry out the other. In another type of problem, the composer does not aim at all at the multiplication of one piece of strategy, but simply endeavours to produce an attractive position of good general strategy, with a nice Key. A number of quotations earlier in this book fulfil these conditions, and I may draw attention to No. 31 with its Ambush Key; the chief variations are:— 1. Kt – Kt7 2. Q × B, 1. Kt – B7 2. B – K3 (Black Interference), 1. B – Q5 2. Kt – K4 (White Interference), 1. P – Q4 2. B – B8 (Open Gate). Or, again, the following, almost a random choice of its pleasant type, in which the total weight of strategy is less than that of No. 31, but good for its light force.

G. Richardson. Observer, May 1925

Mate in 2

Key Q—Kt3, waiting

Black	White	
1	**2**	
Kt—B4, K5	Kt—K5	Interference Unpin
Kt—B5	Q—Kt 7	Interference
B—Kt 7	R—K B4	Self-Block

The other lines are of the simplest type, abandonment of control of squares by Black, and the like. Such a problem is original only in its total effect, not in any particular set of variations, but it often has a charm denied to the "maze of complexity" found in so much modern work.

In passing from the subject of this chapter, I can do no more than refer to the considerable study that has been made of Theme "Loci" and "Spots." A "Spot" is defined as a square occupied by an index piece (often a K) or a position taken up by such a piece in relation to another, and a "Locus" as the total ground comprising all Spots in the theme in question. Take, for example, No. 112, a Task theme. Here the relative positions of the two K's constitute a double Kt's move, and a student might well be interested to discover if the entire theme could be carried out with these pieces in any other relation to each other, nearer or further apart. He would call this double Kt move distance a particular "Spot" of the theme, and the "Locus" would constitute all possible "Spot" distances. Or, again, he might treat the relative position of the Unpinned Q and R as the "Spot," and search for more Spots on this different Locus. More often, the Black K's relative position to thematic units has been taken as a Spot, as in the Half-Pin Theme, where his distance from his Half-pinned assistants, diagonally or laterally, makes a very useful index of originality. It would be a practically impossible task to collect and search through all previous examples of a theme, to avoid anticipations in a new problem, had not some such system as the "Spot" been adopted in filing diagrams.

CHAPTER VIII

CHANGED AND ADDED MATES

Before beginning this Chapter, the student might well read again the relevant definitions and examples (Nos. 8 to 11) given in Chapter II, and refer also to No. 22 (Added Mates) and Nos. 11 and 34 (Changed Mates).

Of all deceptions practised on the solver by the hard-hearted composer, the most deliberate lies in a Key that upsets a set scheme of mates. The elementary process of solving positions that are Complete Blocks is, naturally enough, routine examination of all Black moves and the resulting mates, followed by the endeavour to find a simple waiting move, that will not disturb the equilibrium. Here the art of the composer comes in, with his *suggestio falsi* and *suppressio veri*. The White K, it appears on examination, cannot budge without exposing himself to check, or un-blocking a foolish little Black P; and his allies, on attempting to move, get as much in each other's way as amateurs dancing the Charleston; or else their efforts seem to give undue freedom to Black. The actual Key, in good speci-mens of the type of problem under consideration, should be a surprise, either changing some of the seemingly inevitable mates, or producing new ones. Both these features can occur together, and probably A. C. White is right in deem-ing the most tricky examples to be those in which the Key both changes and adds mates.

One must discriminate between positions that are a Complete Block before the Key, and those in which the composer aims merely at changing the replies to a few prominent Black manoeuvres. The second type does not carry the changed mate idea to its logical conclusion, but it may make quite a solving puzzle, especially to the expert, who hardly expects violent disturbance of play in a position that is obviously not a Block. Moreover, the composer has much more freedom in construction, since he is relieved of the necessity of tying up his pieces to the extreme tightness of the Mutate or Block-Threat. As very little has been done in changed play outside the orthodox Block-Change, though its possible scope is great, I shall give only two examples of what may be called the Free-Change Theme.

No. 119 FREE CHANGE : THREE BLACK CHECKS

G. Guidelli. Observer, June 1920

Mate in 2

Key Kt—B4. Threat KKt—K3

Black	White	
I	2	2
R×P ch	Q×R	KKt—K5
B×P ch	Q×B	Kt×B
Q—K6 ch	P×Q	KKt×Q
(Q×Kt ch)		

Here, and throughout this chapter, the second column gives White's set reply (if any) to a Black move, and the third, his actual mate. It will be evident that the position cannot possibly be, either before or after the Key, a Complete Block, the freedom of the Black forces being much too great, and a change-mate opening does not therefore suggest itself to the solver, familiar, even to contempt, with the Block-Change. I must underline the artistic necessity of the Free Change following *prominent* Black defences; if, for instance, in No. 119 above, the replies to unaggressive moves (such as P – B3) were the only ones altered, the effect would be extremely feeble; the solver has probably failed to notice the set mate for such a move, and does not attempt to keep it in hand. I should add that Andrade has also achieved the task of No. 119, with all three mates *Cross-checks*, on similar lines to No. 138, but as Free Changes. In the Guidelli, nearly all the mates, set and actual, are captures.

In the next example, the Key exchanges the flights Q3 and KB3 for new ones, with the added features of double sacrifice and change of Pin in the mates.

No. 120 FREE CHANGE : FLIGHTS

N. L. Allport. Empire Review, May 1923

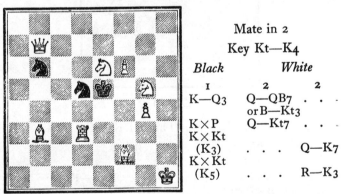

Mate in 2

Key Kt—K4

Black	White	
I	2	2
K—Q3	Q—QB7 . . .	
	or B—Kt3	
K×P	Q—Kt7 . . .	
K×Kt		
(K3)	. . .	Q—K7
K×Kt		
(K5)	. . .	R—K3

We now come to the two main types, the Block-Threat and Mutate. The *Block-Threat* is much the more infrequent

of these, and generally less rich in strategy. The reason, I
think, lies in the fundamental difference in lay-out between
the average Block and Threat problems, and the consequent
difficulty found in the successful amalgamation of the two
species. A few examples follow, in which the essential idea
is blended with well-known themes.

No. 121 BLOCK-THREAT : MULTI-SACRIFICE

G. Heathcote. American Chess Bulletin, 1911

Mate in 2

Key Kt—Q4. Threat R—Kt4

Black	White
1	2
B × Kt	Q—Kt1
P × Kt	Q × QP
K × Kt	Q—Kt4
Q × Kt	Q × RP

The solution of this fine problem is given in straightforward fashion, without showing the changed and added
play; 1. K × Kt and 1. P × Kt yield, of course, added mates,
but whether the other two variations, in which the set mates
remain, can be said to be of the changed type, is a question
of definitions. At least, we can see that the entire machinery

in the diagram—the Black Q focus of her KR2 and B7, and the B that blocks the path to Kt1—is destroyed by the Key.

No. 122 BLOCK-THREAT : FLIGHT-GIVING KEY
J. Stewart. 8th American C.C., 1921

Mate in 2
Key Q—B4
Threat Q—B5

Black	White
1	2
K×P	Kt—B7
K—B4	Q—KB4

No. 123 BLOCK THREAT : BATTERY GIVEN UP
L. Simhovic. Observer, Oct. 1920

Mate in 2
Key Q—K7.
Threat Kt—B2

Black	White	
1	2	2
Q×P ch	K×Q	P×Q
Q—B4 ch	K×Q	Kt×Q
Kt any	K×Kt	(Kt—B2)

Note the abandonment of the set mates following Black Kt moves, without any compensating addition of actual mates. Such "Deducted" play is an unfortunate necessity in many Block-Threats.

L. S. Penrose (revised by B. J. de C. A.). Observer, April 1923

Mate in 2

Key B—B5. Threat Q × R

Black	*White*	
1	2	2
K—Q4	Q—Q4	B × R
Kt—Q6	Q × Kt	Q—B4
Kt—K6 (Kt × B)	Q × P	Q × P

Here also, as in No. 121, one must take *strategy* into consideration in deciding what constitutes a real changed-mate. In No. 124, the same reply follows 1. Kt – K6 (Kt × B in the set play), but mere abandonment of the mating square by the Black Kt is enriched after the Key with Unpin (the theme), and the new strategic element ought to put this variation into the Change class. The reader will come across a number of such moot points in positions of this type, and, until a very exact tabulation has been thought out (it is perhaps impracticable, and probably unnecessary) must rely on his own judgment of them. A sense of surprise at a particular actual mate would not be a bad guide, to begin with.

The next Block Threat given is a highly complex arrangement, with all kinds of new mates due to a set-free Black Q,

and a single change (excluding the threat), following 1 Q –
B4 ch. I may say that Added Mates are much more frequent
in the Block-Threat than the Mutate, as might be expected.

No. 125 BLOCK-THREAT : UNPIN OF BLACK

H. W. Bettmann. Good Companion, April 1921

Mate in 2

Key Q—K3. Threat P—B4

Black	White
1	2
Q×B ⎫ Q—K5 ch ⎭	Q×Q
Q×R ch	Kt×Q
Q×Q ch, etc.	K×Q
Q—B4 ch	R×Q

Deducted play here is 1. P – B3, 2. R × QP and 1. P – R5,
2. K – Kt 4. Note the Try, Q – B4, met by the pinning
defence, Q × R !

The *Mutate* has grown to world-wide popularity during
the last dozen years or so. Previously, only a few sporadic
examples had been published, and even in 1919, when a
collection appeared in "All Change Here," by P. H. Williams
and R. Gevers, probably the total known number did not

exceed 500, now risen, I should estimate, to over 2,000. Hardly any signs of decrease can at present be observed in the rate of output, and it remains a surprise that so much variety can be obtained in a form that has been described as consisting of two problems on one diagram.

By the usual definition of a Mutate, a single changed mate in a Block (both before and after the Key) is sufficient to justify the name, but most composers agree that such a change should have a piquant effect, to justify the machinery. A cumbrous-looking position of many variations, in which the Key alters one or two commonplace mates to others as commonplace, is technically, but not spiritually, a Mutate. A successful light-weight will raise a smile by its quaint attempt at pulling the solver's leg.

No. 126 MUTATE : PIQUANT CHANGE

C. Mansfield. Observer, Dec. 1919

Mate in 2

Key R—KR1.

Black	White	
1	2	2
K—R4	P—Kt4	K—Kt3

P. H. Williams. Morning Post, March, 1918

Mate in 2

Key R—K3

Black	White	
I	2	2
B any	R—QB5	R—Q2

Is there not comedy in the side-step of the Key R, to make a path for his fellow, when the Black B takes the air ? This problem was composed in a London Tube during an air-raid, when Williams was surrounded by a swarm of wondering slum-children, as he very amusingly describes in "All Change Here." These spectators of P. H. W. and his pocket-chessboard were bribed to hold their tongues with a bag of gingernuts. But they continued to discuss him in the most strident tones, and in such words as these: "Look, Alf! 'Ere's the kind gent a-pline *drorfs* wiv hisself." Philip Williams, problemist, musician, and comedian, died in 1922. His chess journalism and his various books, including "The Modern Chess Problem," and "All Change Here," reveal a charming personality.

Treating the Mutate as a pure Task Theme of itself (when humour is rarely conspicuous) we have the record of seven changes in No. 128.

C. Promislo. Boston Transcript, 1919

Mate in 2

Key Q—B5

Black	White	
1	2	2
KKt any	Q—K7	R—K7
Q—B1 ch	R or Q×Q	B—Q8
Q—Kt3	R or Q—B8	Q×Q
Q—Kt 4	R or Q—B8	B×Q
Q—Kt2	R×Q	B×Q
Q×QB	Q—B8	Q×Q
Q×KB	Q—B8	Q×Q

In connection with this variation list, it must be pointed out that when a particular set mate, following several Black moves, is replaced by more than one actual mate, all of these count as Changes. So in No. 128, where five distinct mates replace the set 2. Q – B8; nor does the dualising of this move in three variations (by R – B8) affect the question, and we might sum up the achievement of this problem as "three mates changed to seven." A more satisfying effect is produced, in my opinion, when the number of set and changed mates nearly balance each other, as below.

No. 129 MUTATE : MULTI-CHANGE

J. K. Heydon. Good Companion Folder, April 1921

Mate in 2

Key Kt—K4

Black	*White*	
1	2	2
B—Kt2	Q×Kt	Q×B
Kt any	Q×BP	Kt—B6
P—Kt6	P—B4	Kt—B3
P—B5	KB×P	Q×BP
P×R or Kt	B—QB4	Q—Q6
P—K5	Kt—B4	. . .
K×Kt	. . .	Q—B6

Here five mates are changed to five (counting KB × P and B – QB4, the same piece to the same square, as one mate in the set play) and one is added (such are given last, throughout the chapter) after K × Kt; if, as I suggest, the numbers of set and actual mates were to be summed, the total of eleven in No. 129 is as large as I have experienced. Using this process, we should not, of course, include unchanged mates (such as that following QKt any, in No. 128), or deducted mates, but, on the other hand, we should count the same mate twice over, if it followed one Black move in the set and another in the actual play, changes occurring in both cases. (See No. 131.)

A couple of Mutates follow, in which increased variety is the prominent feature.

No. 130 MUTATE : INCREASED VARIETY
B. J. de C. Andrade. Empire Review, Oct. 1923

Mate in 2

Key R—K6

Black	White	
1	2	2
Kt—B5	Q—K6	Q—K4
Kt else	,,	Q—QR2
K×R	. . .	Q×Kt

A sweet little Miniature, wherein one mate is changed to two, and one is added.

No. 131 MUTATE : INCREASED VARIETY
B. Harley. Bristol Times, Aug. 1925

Mate in 2

Key B×P

Black	White	
1	2	2
P—B6	Q—R4	QP×P
P—K6	Q—Kt4	QP×P
BP×B	. . .	Q—R4
KP×B	. . .	Q—Kt4
K×B	. . .	R—Q5

Two mates are replaced by five. Q – R4 and Kt4 may score as added mates, following, as they do, different Black moves in the set and actual play.

Nearly all the themes given in Chapters IV, V and VI can be combined with the Change-Mate idea. The two examples below show duels between specified White and Black pieces, the next two Key devices, and thereafter the order roughly follows the arrangement of the three chapters mentioned. Very little comment will be added, the headings and solutions speaking for themselves.

No. 132 MUTATE : Q v. Kt
H. L. Schuld. Observer, June 1920

Mate in 2

Key Q—R5

Black	White	
1	2	2
Kt—B1,R1	Q—K4	B—B3
KKt—K2,R5	,,	Q×BP
Kt×B	,,	Q×Kt
Kt×P	,,	Kt×Kt

No. 133 MUTATE : WHITE KT'S v. BLACK KT'S
P. H. Williams. Observer, Oct. 1920

Mate in 2

Key B—Q4

Black	White	
1	2	2
KKt any	Kt—B3	Kt—B6
QKt any	Kt—Q6	Kt—B5

This kind of Key, in which White swings symmetrically across the Black K, and introduces symmetry between the old and new mates, has been christened a "Pendulum" Key by A. C. White.

No. 134 MUTATE : PROVISION AGAINST PIN
J. Warton. Empire Review, Aug. 1926

Mate in 2

Key B—QKt6

Black	White	
1	2	2
R any	R—Kt3	Q—B1

A favourite device, when a change can be introduced by apparently any move of a White piece, forces it to protect the White K, either to prevent check, or more cunningly, as here, to provide against Pin.

No. 135 MUTATE : KEY UNPINS BLACK
W. E. Lester. Empire Review, Jan. 1924

Mate in 2

Key Q—Kt1

Black	White	
1	2	2
B any	Q×QP	Q—KB1
P=Kt	. . .	Q—Kt5
P else	. . .	Q—K4

In the following nine positions, while the *theme* remains unaltered, the thematic mates are changed.

No. 136 MUTATE : FOCAL THEME
B. J. de C. Andrade. Observer, March 1924

Mate in 2

Key Q—Kt6

Black	White	
1	2	2
Q moves	Q—Q5	B—Q6
	or	or
	Q—KB4	Q—Kt5

Before the Key, the Black Q focuses her Q4 and KB5, and after it, her Q3 and KKt4, in opposition to Her White Majesty.   A neat third change, 1. P – K6, 2. Q – KB4 2. P – B4, is worth notice.

No. 137 MUTATE : OPEN GATE
P. F. Kuiper. Good Companion Folder, April 1916

Mate in 2

Key Kt—Q8

Black	White	
1	2	2
R×Kt	Q×Kt	Q—Kt2
B×P	Q—KR8	Kt×B
B else	Q—KR8	Kt—Q7

The Key piece bars the way through the gate to be opened by the Black B, but opens another for the Q. Really a Key Theme, as the Gate Change does not follow the same Black moves. This may be called a *White* Valve (see No. 117).

No. 138 MUTATE : TWO BLACK CROSS-CHECKS
B. J. de C. Andrade and F. F. L. Alexander. Observer, July 1923

Mate in 2

Key Q—B8

Black	White	
1	2	2
Q—Kt4,	Kt (B7)	Kt(K6)
R5 ch	—Kt5	—Kt5
Q—R6 ch	Kt—Q6	Kt—B5

A task that had baffled composers for many a year.

No. 139 MUTATE : GRIMSHAW INTERFERENCE
L. S. Penrose. Observer, Aug. 1920

Key K—R5

Black	White	
1	2	2
R—Kt7	B—B3	Q—B3
B—Kt7	Q×P(K3)	Q—Kt4

Different mates follow the mutual interference of the Black R and B. There is one other changed and one added, but

137

I shall now in general specify only those relevant to the particular theme.

No. 140 MUTATE : WHITE AND BLACK INTERFERENCE

L. S. Penrose. Observer, Feb. 1922

Mate in 2

Key Q × QRP

Black	White	
1	2	2
R—B4	Kt × P	Kt—Kt6
R—Q5	Kt—K3	Q—QB7
B—Q5	. . .	B × P

A curious mixture of interference play occurs, the Grimshaw (R – B4 and B – Q5) being introduced by the Key, with a changed and an added mate, while the White Interference set after 1. R – Q5 becomes a Black. The Key also deducts, rather violently, the set mate after 1. P – R3! The intensity with which chess problems are studied by their devotees is shown by the fact that many composers confine their efforts to the Two-mover, and a few (of whom Penrose is one, with his change-mates) to a particular type of that length.

No. 141 MUTATE : BLACK UNPINS WHITE

C. E. Kemp. Observer, June 1925

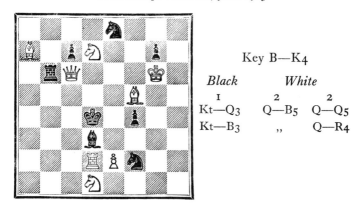

Key B—K4

Black	White	
1	2	2
Kt—Q3	Q—B5	Q—Q5
Kt—B3	,,	Q—R4

No. 142 MUTATE : BLACK SELF-PIN

J. Stewart. Good Companion Folder, April 1919

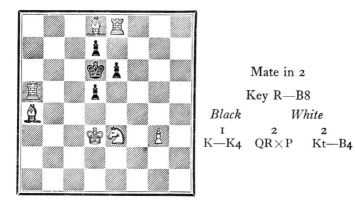

Mate in 2

Key R—B8

Black	White	
1	2	2
K—K4	QR×P	Kt—B4

The Pin-Mate feature, due to the KP, becomes dependent on the P on Q4.

No. 143 MUTATE : HALF-PIN

C. Promislo. Eighth American Chess Congress, 1921

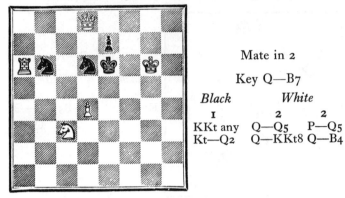

Mate in 2

Key Q—B7

Black	White	
1	2	2
KKt any	Q—Q5	P—Q5
Kt—Q2	Q—KKt8	Q—B4

The complete Half-Pin change has never, before or after, been done so neatly; the full theme occurs in both the set and actual play.

No. 144 MUTATE : BATTERY CHANGED

C. G. Watney. Observer, Dec. 1919

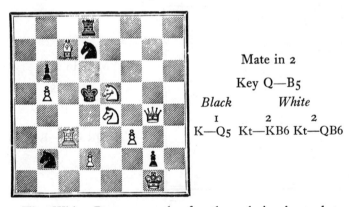

Mate in 2

Key Q—B5

Black	White	
1	2	2
K—Q5	Kt—KB6	Kt—QB6

The White Battery on the fourth rank is changed to another on the fifth.

No. 145 MUTATE: WHITE BATTERY ABANDONED

B. Harley. Chess Amateur, 1916

Mate in 2

Key Q—B2

Black	White	
1	2	2
Kt—Q3, K2	K × Kt	Kt—Q6
KKt any	K—B5	Q × P
KtP × P	K—Q7	Kt × P

Compare this with the Block-Threat, No. 123.

No. 146 MUTATE : WHITE BATTERY INTRODUCED

W. E. Lester. Observer, March 1923

Mate in 2

Key Q—R5

Black	White	
1	2	2
B × P	Q × B	K × P
Kt—B5	Kt—Q3	K × Kt
Kt—Q6	Kt × Kt	K × Kt
KKt any	Q—Kt3	K—Q4

Quite elegant, contrasted with the cumbersome setting of the reverse theme in the previous problem.

No. 147 MUTATE : THREE P PROMOTIONS

B. J. de C. Andrade and C. G. Watney. Observer, April 1923

Mate in 2

Key Kt (Kt5)—Q4

Black	White	
1	2	2
Kt×R	P×Kt (Kt)	P×Kt (Q)
Kt—Kt2	P—K8 (Q)	P—K8 (Kt)
R—Q1	P×R (Kt)	P×R (Q)

An amazing Task Record this. The reader can see for himself that the only changes possible on a mating move lie between the choice of Q or Kt.

The Echo Theme has a special application in the Mutate. In other types of the Two-Move problem, it is the actual mates that imitate each other, but here we have great additional possibilities in the echo of set mates by the actual mates, in distinct variations.

No. 148 MUTATE : ECHO CHANGES

B. J. de C. Andrade. Observer, Nov. 1922

Mate in 2

Key Q—QKt3

Black	White	
1	2	2
Kt—B6	Q—B5	P—Q3
Kt—Q6	P—B3	Q—Q5
KKt else	P—Q3	P—B3

The first pair of variations are most curiously interwoven, the set and actual replies to symmetrical Black moves echoing each other in a bewildering way. For instance, the actual 2. P – Q3 echoes the set P – B3 in its companion variation, and a similar relation holds between the Q mates. The third variation shows an echo between set and actual mates, after the same Black move.

In No. 149 there are two pairs of variations with the effect of cross-symmetry displayed in No. 148, while the Keys of both problems are of the Pendulum species.

No. 149 MUTATE : ECHO CHANGES

B. Harley. All Change Here! 1919

Mate in 2.   Key R—B4

Black	*White*	
I	2	2
P—B3	B—K6	Kt—Kt6
P—K3	Kt—B6	B—B6
P—Kt6	P—B4	Kt—B3
P—B6	Kt—K3	P—K4

For the Echo feature, see also No. 138. A few special ideas complete this chapter.

No. 150 MUTATE : P×P *e.p.* CHANGE

B. Harley. Observer, Oct. 1925

Mate in 2

Key R×P

Black	White	
1	2	2
P—B4 ch	KtP×P	KP×P
	e.p.	*e.p.*

In changing the *en passant* capture from one P to another, the curious point arises that a Dual mate is a thematic necessity after the single square advance of the doomed Black P. The double leap of the P must *force* a reply that the single-square move does not, in order to make the *en passant* change distinctive.

No. 151 MUTATE : THREE CHANGES DUE TO ONE BLACK P

W. Langstaff. Observer, Jan. 1924

Mate in 2

Key R—B8

Black	White	
1	2	2
P—Q3	Q×QP	Q—K3
P—Q4	Q—Q6	B—Q7
P×B	Q—Kt5	Q×BP

In No. 152 the point lies in the try, Castles, assuming that the solver regards such a manoeuvre as within the rules. Analysis of previous play makes it evident that the White K must have moved in the hypothetical game, to let in his rival; Castling is therefore "off the map."

No. 152 MUTATE : "CAN'T CASTLE"
B. Harley. Chess Amateur, May 1922

Mate in 2

Key K—Q1

Black	White	
1	2	2
P × BP	B × P	K—B2
K × P	. .	B × P

And now we have a delightful Castling Mutate.

No. 153 MUTATE : CASTLES
G. Stuart Green. Observer, Oct. 1929

Mate in 2

Key Castles

Black	White	
1	2	2
B × BP	Kt—B1	R × B
B × RP	R × B	Kt × RP

145

Composers of Changed-Play problems have found themselves compelled to modify the rigid theory of Economy of Force (treated in the next Chapter). While they avoid as much as possible units required only in the set play, circumstances are generally too strong for them, and hardly a Mutate of any complexity will lack a few "Duds," as they are called. All things, however, and all moods being possible to the Problemist, he may occasionally glorify the Dud, even to the extent of creating a "spoof" White Q. So please pardon the perpetration that ends the chapter.

No. 154 MUTATE : DUD THEME

B. Harley. Chess Amateur, 1917

Mate in 2

Key R—K4

Black	White	
1	2	2
Kt—B5, Kt6	K × Kt	Kt × P (B6)
QKt any	K—K3	Kt—K3
QP any	K—K2	B—B4

CHAPTER IX

CONSTRUCTION

The principles of construction of a chess problem can almost be summed up in one word—Economy. But this word must be sub-divided, like all Gaul, into three parts: Economy of Idea, Economy of Force in presenting that idea, and Economy of Play.

Economy of Idea. It is a mistake to drag trifling and non-thematic variations into a problem. These are called "Fringe-variations," or "Fringes," and are often added by inexperienced composers who do not realise that the quality, and not the quantity of play, is the important thing. The problem art is a very controversial subject, and there is no uniform standard by which one can define a Fringe to a certainty. My own creed is given, for what it is worth.

Any variation that arises from force that is necessary to the composer's idea is justified. It would be a travesty of Theme-Economy to cut out a side-line, by putting on more force. I would, on occasion, rearrange the theme-force, or even slightly increase it, to work in another mate. Such *automatic* variety is found in most problems, and will not offend the taste of many people.

The next diagram exemplifies my notion of a bad Fringe. I want the reader to turn to No. 38 in this book. The variations are

| 1. Q any | 2. R—QB3; | 1. K—Q1, |
| 2. B—Kt6 | 1. B any | 2. Q×Q |

The R's Key-square is governed by the Black Q check, which it allows and awaits. The flight yields a Pin-Mate, and the Black B an elementary abandonment of guard. Now, with regard to the two lines outside the main idea of the Cross-Check, I should never, I believe, consider a K flight variation as a fringe; here, moreover, the flight comes under White control by an Open Gate in the main play, and adds point to it.

The Black B has two necessary uses, block of a square in the K's field, and guard of its Q; its variation is quite automatic, and a desirable makeweight in a rather sparsely-varied problem.

In the following diagram I have turned the late Donald Mackay's problem (No. 38) upside down (I hope his gentle shade will forgive me) in order to add the fringe line, after the Key (R – Q6) by 1. P – B6, 2. Kt – Q3 mate.

No. 38A FRINGE VARIATION

Key R—Q6

1. P—B6,   2. Kt—Q3

This Knight has nothing whatever to do with either the lay-out of the Theme-Force, or the Control-Force of the Black K's field. Its object, to give mate after the P's elementary abandonment of a square, is palpable, for it cannot make a Try, nor can it have a possible use to prevent a Cook. It is a Fringe-Unit, pure and simple. I have no doubt that some beginners would add, to No. 38A, a White B on QR7 and a Black Kt on QKt3, so as to get a double checkmate by Kt – Q3, when the Black Kt moves; which gives me the chance of emphasising the fact that to complicate a variation is not necessarily to improve it. I have too often seen a simple, natural variation artificialised beyond recognition by a novice who has just discovered such things as Batteries. Even the complete Half-pin line is unjustified, if it merely replaces two straightforward mates, and contains no strategy that harmonises with the rest of the play.

In general, a composer must rely on his taste and judgment, natural and acquired, as to the kind of play he should avoid in a particular problem. There are light-weights and heavy-weights, but one should avoid a position that gives the impression of a cumbrous addition of a complex variation (or more than one) to an essentially slight scheme. There will, however, always be border-line cases, in which the composer himself, let alone the critics, cannot be sure if he has sinned too greatly against Unity of Play. Speaking quite generally, I would put on Black force (rarely White) to add a variation of respectable strategy, such as a Self-Block or Self-Inter-ference (as a minimum) in almost any problem. But some critics disagree. The Black Kt on KKt2 in No. 43 has been denounced as a fringe. This Kt adds an Unpin of the White Q by the interference 1. Kt – B4 2. Q – K4, and seems to me to go well with the two similar Interference-Unpins by the other Black Kt. The variation has, it is true, nothing to do with the Black Kt Wheel, unmasking the R (K2) upon the threat square, but it is legitimate to consider that the problem illustrates two Themes, the Wheel mingled with Unpin of White. Apart from this consideration, I believe, as I indicated above, that the piece in question amply justifies its existence by producing a variation of what may be called "secondary" strategy. All this shows very clearly what differences of opinion can arise in the problem art.

Another way in which a breach of Theme-Economy can arise lies in the unnecessary repetition of a mate. In the usual way of thinking, problemists reckon variations by the different mates forced upon White, to carry out his contract. On this basis, there is no point whatever in adding force to a position, so that a second Black move may introduce a mate that already occurs. Most composers would, I think, actually prefer each of their mates to follow one Black move only, especially in dramatic and surprising variations. Take, for example, one of those highly complex lines in Chapter VII, where cross-checking, pinning and the like, are all bound together in one variation. Would not such an aristocratic defence seem a little humbled if a poor relation, a plain cover of the threat square, forced the same mate? These things cannot always be helped, and naturally there are plenty of themes, such as the Focal, in which several Black moves yield one mate only, but only in special circumstances will a composer add units, just to repeat a mate. Here follows a very deliberate example by a great composer.

No. 155 BLACK DUALS

V. Marin. Spanish National Tourney, 1919

Mate in 2

Key Q—K8. Threat Q—K7

The theme is the Interference-Unpin of the White KR, which goes to two squares, capturing the P after 1. Kt – B6, and to R2 after no less than five Black defences, R – Kt2, Kt – B3, Kt – K5, P – Q4 and P – K5. The strategic defect on Black's part is of an identical nature in all five moves, and only one Variation can be allowed, in my opinion, to arise. I should call such additions of alternative defences Ornaments or Embroidery. I confess I am doubtful as to the justification of this emphatic underlining of an Unpin. From one point of view, repetitions of strategy, yielding the same mate, might be called Black Duals, or unwanted Options of the defence.

There are two cases in which identical White mates (moves of the same piece to the same square) are usually considered to yield distinct variations. First, when the mated K is on different squares; secondly, when elements of separate strategy arise. The next example shows both cases rather well.

No. 156 DISTINCT MATES

E. J. Eddy. West Sussex Gazette, 1929

Mate in 2

Key Q—Q1. Threat R—KB4

If 1. B×R or K×P,   2. QKt—B5
If 1. R×R or R—B2,   2. Kt—B6

In the first line of variations, the K is mated on Kt5 and R5, and one could argue (to help out what would otherwise be a tame distinction), that K × P, necessitating a double-check reply, contains different defensive ideas to 1. B × R, when 2. QKt – B5 merely shuts off the Black R. In the second variation, 1. R × R self-pins, and White has only to shut off the Black B, whereas 1. R – B2 defeats the threat by cutting off the White B's line, and the reply shuts off both Black R and B.

Finally, there is the case of addition of force to enrich a particular variation, which is much more frequently seen than Marin's idea of multiplying a form of Black strategy in a single line. No. 127 gives an example. Moves of the Black Kt on R8 interfere with his R focus of QKt5 and KKt7, introducing the identical pair of mates (Kt × KtP and R × B) that follow moves of the R. The strategy becomes Black Interference on focal lines, which, I suppose, would be considered some enrichment of the plain upset of the focus. It pleases many solvers, but I am doubtful if this sort of thing is otherwise justified, unless it harmonises with the main theme. (See also the Black KKt in No. 50.)

Economy of Play. I deal with this, for convenience, before Economy of Force. White Duals, or the choice of alternatives in reply to a particular Black move, were defined in Chapter II. In the present section, the word is used in its general sense of any number of options, and not only a double one.

There have been two absolutely opposed Schools of thought on the subject. The Bohemians, following some of the Germans, held that as long as you could force the variations you want (certain Black moves compelling distinct White replies) it was of no particular consequence that other Black moves could be met by two, three or more replies. You had your main body of play, and if Black cared to go outside it, and (as it were) select a feeble defence, it was not the business of the composer to prevent him by adding extra units, Black or White. Economy of Force, in short, was more important than Economy of Play. The great importance attached by this School to the Model Mate was, naturally, a contributory cause of its decision. The other side, the Anglo-Americans and some of the Continentals, were fiercely opposed to Duals of any kind, especially to those of the Major variety. Their argument might be put thus. It is the composer's business to control the whole of the play, not only his thematic variations. The pieces are all his puppets and he must see that they do not misbehave themselves. This School preferred Economy of Play to rigid Economy of Force in the Two-move problem.

Both Schools of thought have had to abandon their original ideals, under the inexorable pressure of events. It has become a difficult task to compose a novel Two-mover on Model Mates lines. Possible arrangements are limited, and have been so thoroughly explored, that very little remains to be done. The strict Bohemian school must be content with the glories of its past. On the other hand, the rise of the complex variation, which has given new life to the moribund Two-mover of a generation ago, has compelled the Anti-Dualists to reconsider their position. They had to answer this question. Is a fine theme-combination to be thrown overboard, never to see the light of day, because a Dual cannot by any means be eradicated? The diehards stuck to their guns, and when such positions came up for judgment before them cast them aside, as beyond the pale, and often awarded their honours to trite but correct arrangements. There is no doubt whatever that such a masterpiece as Mansfield's No. 46 would have suffered this fate at the hands of many of the judges of the past. The Duals after K – K4 (by 2. Kt × Kt or Kt – B7) and moves of the QKt outside the thematic variations (by 2. Kt – QKt5 or B4) would have struck horror to the souls of people to whom a single Dual was anathema.

The modern composer does not like Duals, but he compromises; he has to. He will probably stop a Dual if it costs him a little extra Black force (he hates adding White force that does no work in the real play, as my next section on Economy of Force will expound). This Black force must, however, stop the particular Dual in all its ramifications, or he will not bother about it. Looking again at No. 46, you will see that Mansfield could have blocked Black's QR4 and 6 with P's; but the identical Dual would follow Kt – Kt3 or 7. So he rightly lets it go; it all constitutes a single Dual, and whether it follows four or two Black moves is of the slightest importance.

As an alternative to the direct addition of units for the prevention of Duals, it is often advisable to rearrange your force, and even to increase it, so long as your extra pieces have a use in the real play. For example, a recalcitrant White unit, holding a couple of squares in the Black K's field, which insists on introducing a Dual, may give place to two of its fellows, each holding one of the two squares, when the Dual (we assume) disappears. A good deal of this juggling with strict economy of force is done in the modern problem, to get the play perfectly clean, so long as a plausible, if not absolutely logical reason can be given for every unit on the board. Though it may be said to rob Peter to pay Paul, it seems to me to be justifiable tactics, when used with discretion. I suppose I must add the rather obvious remark that a composer, on finding a Major Dual line (a mate that is not forced in any of his arranged variations) will, first of all, endeavour to introduce it as a real variation. Should he find that the added strategy is not worth the force that he has to employ, only then will he consider its eradication, bearing in mind that a Dual of the Major variety, containing *unwanted* strategy, is considered more objectionable than its Minor brother, which merely repeats mates that occur in the true play. Nor does one care for a Minor Dual that follows striking Black strategy. One feels, instinctively, that the reply to a Black check, to take one instance, ought not to be dualised. The composer *seems* to have missed a chance of working in a respectable variation, even if in reality the Dual could not be helped. This is a surface view, I admit, but the points of a problem that jump to the eye, as well as the depths concealed beneath the shallows, are of importance.

The question of adding force, solely to prevent Duals, is dealt with in the next Section. Here are a few rather haphazard remarks, to complete a subject that has lost the vital interest it had for our fathers. Duals by choice of promotion of a P have never been considered serious. In the Two-move, White cannot, of course, set up stalemate on his second move, so that, if his mating P can become a R or B, it is obvious that a Q will always be an alternative choice. The issue, therefore, may be said to lie between the Kt and the other pieces collectively, and one or other of these two options ought to be forced, in order to avoid a Dual. Next, it has been maintained that Duals are more serious in a Block position than in a Threat problem. I have never seen a convincing reason for this theory. Again, some hold that a Dual in reply to a Black move that defeats the threat is more objectionable than one due to blind stupidity, as it were, that disregards the threat altogether. The theory is that Duals should be due to absolute accidents, and should not follow any deliberate manoeuvre by Black. This argument tends to the conclusion that Duals in a Block, where Black has no threat to defeat, are not so important, after all!

Such minutiae do not much trouble the modern composer. Most of us keep an open mind on the subject and consider each case by itself. We generally take some trouble to stop a single Dual in an otherwise correct problem. We certainly dislike Major Duals. I will add my own prejudice against Duals that arise from an extremely restricted Black force. If, out of four possible moves (let us say), one of these allows a Dual, there seems to be too large a *proportion* of inaccuracy. What is one to say about Duals in the *set* play only of a Mutate or Block-Threat? Are "Set-Duals," worked out by the Key, to count as flaws at all? I, for one, regard the arranged play in a Changed-Variation Theme as only of less importance than the real play. Moreover, a Set-Dual has its own peculiar disadvantage in its indication of a Key that will abolish it. It may be a sign-post in the very type of problem that calls most for deception. Nor do I like a "Thematic" Dual, that is, one that displays the kind of strategy of the general theme. In No. 58, 1. R – B4 allows, by Black Interference, either 2. Q – R4 or R – R4.

Everything, good or bad, connected with problems, seems to have been thematised at some time or another. Mansfield, in a light-hearted moment, has thus glorified the Dual, by a Key of five threats, all of which are separately forced by Black replies. A diabolically perverse Task, that gives me the occasion of saying that the Dual of a Double (or Multiple) Threat need not be the worse for its inclusion, as it were, in the Key. It is the Key that loses merit by the aggression of the Double Threat.

Economy of Force. The Composer, having determined upon all the effects he wishes to produce, should try to find the most economical setting. This is a question of technique, evolved from a nucleus of natural ability, and improved by practice. The difference between the expert and the tyro is nowhere else shown so emphatically as in the process of cutting down the force, necessary to express an idea, to its bare bones. Economy of Force has nothing to do with the size of a problem. A feather-weight, even a miniature, may contain bad breaches of economy, while a cruiser-weight, with almost every unit on the board, may be absolutely economical; or, at any rate, as economical as the particular scheme will allow. It is true that, *generally speaking*, one expects greater variety or complexity from a large force than from a small one. But there are many cases, such as the Tuxen Theme (No. 102), which are expensive in units by their nature.

There will always be differences of opinion among even the most skilful composers, and perhaps the expression "Economy of Force" will never convey the same meaning in all circumstances to any two of them. Here are two points of general agreement.

(1) Of pieces of the same colour, one of a lower value is to be preferred to a higher.

(2) White economy is more important than Black.

(1) Part of the composer's idea may be close Tries, and occasions may arise when he considers himself justified in

using the more mobile of two units. The White Q in Williams' No. 127 could be a B, without affecting the real play in the slightest degree. All composers have to meet, on occasion, the awkward situation of a fine set of variations, with possibly an excellent Key (from the theoretical point of view) but with no shadow of a plausible Try. And it can be argued that the frequent presence in Change-Mate themes of "dud" force (units that have use only in the set play) which is admitted by nearly all exponents of this form of problem to be thematically justified, makes out a case for the inclusion of duds in any and every problem. Bonavia Hunt has even thematised the dud, and introduced false Half-Pin lines, never to be exploited, into non-change problems. I must confess that this glorification of the "Subtracted Mate" does not appeal to me, and seems to be allied to the ancient process of "dressing the board," or adding units where and how you pleased, for the purpose of distracting the solver's eye. My opinion is that any increase of force, for introducing the evasive quality of difficulty into a problem, should be used with great discretion, and rather by the substitution of units of more or less equivalent power than by the blatant addition or aggrandisement of pieces. I have also seen a Black unit's power increased, not to create difficulty, but to add importance to a White unit. A pinned Black Q has been substituted for a R (which would introduce exactly the same play) in order to enhance the function of the pinning White unit. The argument, upheld by a great master of the art, seems to be artificial.

We now come to the general question of the use of alternative pieces in guarding squares, preventing Cooks and Duals and so on; that is, force that is not earmarked for the theme machinery. The relative values do not always follow those of the game, in the eyes of the problemist. The composer likes to keep down the number of his pieces, to prevent a heavy appearance, and to maintain a high average of mobility of the units employed. Exactly what compromise he makes, between Force-value and the number of units, depends on individual feeling, which will vary even in the same composer from time to time, for no very apparent reason. He will be influenced in his options by many factors, such as a heightening of the effect of the Key, creation of near Tries, prevention of Duals, and others. Usually, dealing with pieces of the same colour, he will substitute one guard-piece for two when the disparity of total force is not too striking. For instance, a Q will often be used instead of two minor pieces, or even for a minor piece and a P (always, of course, for the full equivalent of two R's, circumstances permitting). A minor piece, or even a R, will be substituted for two P's; even occasionally for one, if some feature of the problem is enhanced thereby.

(2) The relative importance of White economy of force in comparison with Black is deeply engrained in most composers' consciousness. It may be just a relic from the teaching of a past generation; perhaps it is dimly connected with the theory of economical White force in the mate, that still holds a large part of the field in the three-move problem. Perhaps it comes from the chess-player's influence on the art (which is greater than is generally believed); in his desire to see the forces evened up, to "give Black a chance." From his pleased surprise when he sees, as he sometimes does, a tiny White force put to rout the most enormous Black battalions. The game-player loves Sacrifice (the crudest of the problemist's tricks) and he regards such a problem as a position in a game, in which the winner must have wallowed in his favourite pursuit. Anyhow, argue as one may (and I should never be surprised if a hyper-modern problemist were to argue to the opposite effect, and find excellent reasons that the White force should be as large as possible) the fact remains that nearly all of us are agreed that quite considerable Black force should take the place of small White force, for the purpose of preventing Cooks and Duals, and very generally for guarding squares in the Black K's field. This last use is, however, influenced a little by the desire for keeping an open position round the K, and we sometimes find a White P, for example, taking the place of a blocking Black P and relieving a too-crowded collection of units.

Composers dislike especially *outlying* White force (not bearing on the Black K's field, directly or in a Battery), unless it has some deceptive object. An outlying White P, controlling a square just beyond the field, will often indicate that the Black K is to be allowed to walk out in its direction, when a flight-giving Key loses its element of surprise. Quite large Black force, in size or number, may be preferred to a single White P that is not necessary to the real play. No general rule can be given, and composers differ a great deal in their feeling on the subject, but the principle is widely admitted.

The desire for Naturalness of Position (*i.e.* from the game-player's point of view) has some small effect on the treatment of Economy of Force. Modern Composers will certainly not attempt to even up the White and Black forces, but they try to avoid ugly clusters of pieces and P's, especially collections of P's on one file, whether of the same or different colours, which would make the hypothetical game that produced the problem position rather more peculiar than usual. What are called "Open Positions" are desirable. The force is spread out over the board, if it is practicable, and lines of many pieces, whether on ranks, files or diagonals, are avoided. All this helps to make a problem look attractive. Every position can be reversed from left to right without the slightest difference to the play (unless Castling is involved). This process changes the colours of the squares, and as pieces (especially White pieces) print more clearly on White squares than on Black, it is often worth while to adopt the arrangement that brings the majority of the White force upon White squares. The White K, if he cannot be introduced into the play, and cannot stop a Cook or a Dual, nor make a Try, is usually put down on his Castling line—a barefaced concession to the game-player.

I shall now review some of the early chapters of this book in their relation to Construction.

THE KEY

The Key may be in the composer's mind throughout his

work. A few composers say that they invariably begin a problem with both Key and variation-play in their minds. Such a counsel of perfection is beyond most of us, and as often as not we build up our variations, with mental notes of certain alternative arrangements, finally adding the best Key we can find. In some themes, the Key is so much a part and parcel of the idea (the Change-Mate occurs at once) that construction must naturally begin with it. Flight-square and Sacrificial Themes, Unpinning of Black and Self-Pin of White, Nowotnys, Bristols and Anti-Bristols are obviously Key-Themes. In such cases, thematics Keys are a necessity; in many others, they are very desirable, in particular those that feature Black aggression. I am never much intrigued with a Black Check that is seen in the diagram. If it is only a side-line, nobody can object, but I do feel strongly that, as a theme, Black Checks should be introduced by the Key. And so with Pins or captures of White. Beginners love to display big White units in positions of *en prise*. This should be done by the Key. Otherwise, in nine cases out of ten, the imminent danger to the mating force merely indicates the process of play. In some other themes, mostly concerned with accidental Black strategy, the Key should not be "thematic." A Key that completes a Half-Pin line, for example, is, at best, provisional to a high degree, and should be avoided. Mansfield's No. 89 is one of the very few problems of the first rank that has such a Key, and readers will notice that there is ample compensation in the flight (and Black Check) that is given, as well as in the sacrifice of the Key-piece. Very many Keys have to be compromises, and one must balance the pro's against the con's. In Chapter VI, in connection with No. 87, I give some opinions on Thematic Keys.

In the last few years there has been a reaction from a period of rather prosaic Keys, which were due perhaps to the ubiquity of the Half-Pin theme. One composer, in especial, J. A. Schiffmann, came to the front with a remarkable series of problems, that one and all have pointed openings.

J. A. Schiffmann. Brisbane Courier, 1929

Mate in 2

Key R—Q5. Threat B—B4

Black	White
1	2
B—K4	R—Kt5
R—K4	Kt—B8
R—Q3	Kt—B4
B—Q3	R—Q3

These four variations show the Double Grimshaw Interference (see No. 61) using two Black R's and one B. Also (and the combination is an unique achievement) the Key is a Nowotny (see No. 32) obstructing a Black R and B at their point of intersection, and yielding the two typical mates, B – B4 and Q – B3. The second mate does not occur as one of two double threats, which is meritorious in a Nowotny Two-mover. We cannot call this Key strictly thematic, since a Nowotny has, *per se*, nothing to do with a Grimshaw, but we can surely feel that this mingling of White Interference of Black with Black Self-Interference is not only diabolically clever, but seems to turn the natural aggressiveness of the Nowotny into an actual merit.   Looking at this problem (and others) we have it forced upon us that all the conventions about good and bad Keys (and we may extend this to everything else in a problem) can be successfully broken at times by composers of genius.   Schumann told his fellow-critics of a century ago, enraged at Chopin's harmonic innovations, especially his use of consecutive double-fifths, that they could learn an infinite deal from the study of that composer's works, and about consecutive fifths most of all.

VARIATIONS

The simplest kind of variation is one in which a Black unit (whether it takes a haphazard choice in a Block, or deliberately defeats a threat) allows mate by abandoning control of a square.   In this elementary class I should also put the capture of a White unit, allowing mate by recapture, and a K move into a simple mating-net.   Positions made up entirely, or almost entirely, of such variations can hardly be exhausted.   They show no outstanding points, and scarcely submit to any classification, so that it is difficult to decide on their novelty, which exists (if at all) in the total effect and not in any one variation.   Such problems will, however, continue to be composed and published in considerable numbers, and will give pleasure to the unsophisticated solver and occasionally even to the expert, jaded with the complex "variation-net."   One might perhaps liken a composition of this kind to an old Italian opera, with its simple graces, in contrast to the contrapuntal devices of Wagner, the poly-thematist.   A reasonably light and attractive appearance, and a neat Key, should be features of these unpretentious efforts.   The play, moreover, should be "clean," that is to say, free from Duals, or almost entirely so.   I quote a successful example of this type, in which success is not easily to be achieved, simple though the result may appear. The composer has deliberately worked for his effect, and has wisely avoided the addition of a single complex variation, which would appear quite out of place—an orchid in a bunch of primroses.

No. 158 PRIMARY VARIATIONS

G. C. Holroyd. Observer, August 1926

Mate in 2

Key Kt—KKt6

Apart from the Self-Block by 1. B – K5, allowing 2. Q – Q7, and the opening of the White Battery upon QB6 by moves of the mating QKt, every variation is of the primary type mentioned above. Black is obliged, after the waiting Key, to give up control of one or other of the numerous mating squares. This sort of problem should be studied by young composers first of all, in my opinion. So they will acquire something of the art of Unity of Construction, the combining of the pieces in an orderly and economical way, before coming to more intricate ideas.

Rather more advanced (secondary) strategy is shown in the Self-Block variation (No. 52). White induces his opponent to close an exit for his K, and the theme introduces two squares (instead of one, as in the primary variations) for consideration; the square to be blocked and the mating square. The "Antiform" of the Self-Block (to use a word recently coined by Palatz and Mongredien in their book of that title) is, of course, Flight-Obtaining (No. 40). Open-

Gate or Line-Evacuation variations (No. 51), Unmasking Defences (No. 43) and discovery of a White Battery upon a flight-square (as in No. 158 above), may also be classed together. They add a *line of play* to the mating idea, and seem to me to have about as much strategic merit as Self-Block and Flight-Obtaining variations.

Black Interference (No. 58) involves two line-directions, the crisis occurring at a junction, and takes the next step in my rough classification of merit. A little more complex is the usual form of White Interference (No. 53), when a Self-Block is joined to a line of intersection. Black Checks, bringing the White K into critical play, are also advanced tactics, especially the Cross-Check (No. 46).

The reader will understand that every additional square, or line of play, that is introduced into a variation in a thematic way (influencing the play, defensive or attacking) increases the complexity, and therefore, from the strategic point of view, the worth of the variation. He may be referred to No. 97, and my analysis of its main elements.

Pins of White, or Unpins of White by Black, are advanced strategy, also giving the White K a leading motif. Unpin of White by *himself*, which can only be effectively done by the Key, is of course of no merit. Self-Pin of Black, whether directly or by a Half-Pin line, and Unpin of Black are high on my list. All these have been illustrated in the previous Chapters on themes. It is interesting to the student of human nature (as well as of problems) to see how problem themes follow the fashion of the moment. Thirty years ago, it was the Cross-Check that ran amok through the ranks of the great technicians and their imitators. The Half-Pin was the next craze, with the Change-Mate accompanying on this side of the Atlantic. At present, as I have said before and gladly repeat, composers appear to be concentrating on "snappy" Key-themes. What will come next, and what will happen to the Two-Move Problem in the distant future? No one can even guess. One fantastic suggestion that I

made to Alain C. White a few years ago was the Thematic
Cook, shown below.

No. 159 THEMATIC COOKS

B. Harley. Observer, August 1923

Mate in 2, in three ways

Keys: (a) Kt – K4. Mutate, with one mate added and
three changed.

(b) B – B7. Mutate, with two mates changed.

(c) R – R6. Block-Threat, with three new mates,
including the threat.

I must confess that my subscription to this setting, on its
original appearance, was "Mate in two," my main purpose
being the separation of my solvers' scores. Mr. White
deemed the problem an example of Fairy Chess (the generic
name for play that goes outside the rules of the game) but
one could argue (perhaps perversely) that alternative methods
of completing White's contract merely make a problem more
like the average game of chess.

After this digression, I had better come back to earth with
a few observations on the Changed Mate Theme. I like

plenty of play, both set and new. The neat little traps have nearly all been fully exploited, it seems, and changes in secondary strategy offer the best hope of originality. The real play should be superior, in this respect, or at any rate not inferior to the set play. Positions which show an extremely constricted Black force gave pleasure in the past, when the "change" idea was a novelty, but will not obtain much approbation in the eyes of the experienced modern critic. A free-moving White force is also very desirable. There will probably be a good number of tries, and if the Black units are also given elbow-room the position does not at once suggest a Mutate. After all, the basic object of this type of problem should be deception, and not merely an exercise in changed play.

CHAPTER X

COMPOSING

The art of composing chess problems can be taught to just about the same degree as any other art. That is to say, not very far. To make a first-rate original problem, you must have an adequate technique, a knowledge of what has been already achieved, ideas, and . . . luck. Technique is a matter of practice. There must be a continual effort to get the last ounce of play out of every one of your units. All alternative arrangements, however fantastic they may appear at first sight, must be examined, until you find yourself up against an impossible objection. And you must criticize your work as fiercely as if it were an alien product. The great majority of problems that appear in print, apart from quotations of prize-winners and famous old chestnuts, are not of this standard. They give sufficient pleasure for their day, but will not live in the memories or collections of connoisseurs. Their good points, in Key or variations, are often discounted, in the eyes of the expert, by a wasteful setting, with feeble and unnecessary by-play; or, if an inexperienced composer has chanced to hit on a really neat rendering, in most cases he has reproduced, with slight if any difference, a position by an old master. A would-be composer ought to possess a small problem library, which should include "The Good Companion Two-Mover," by George Hume and A. C. White, and "Simple Two-Move Themes," by F. Bonner Feast and A. C. White (both in the

A. C. White series), and he should watch the prize-winning positions of current Tourneys. So he will learn the trend of modern composition. This he must know, for even the most daring heretic (as he may become) has to be acquainted with the tenets that he outrages.

My third qualification for great composing, the inventive faculty, is the rarest. Without new ideas, the finest technician has to follow a blazed trail, widening the path by his record "task" achievements, or embellishing it with graceful ornamentation, according to his temperament. A very few composers combine good inventive powers with severe self-criticism and artistic restraint. Most often, originality of outlook seems to go with a certain carelessness of constructive detail, or a facile outpouring of a great quantity of trifling productions. Such generalities, however, apply to all the arts. Let us trace a typical problem composing career (not my own).

It will start at an early age, when the chess faculty is most rapidly developed. In this respect the problemist resembles the chess-player; all the world-champions, from Morphy to Alekhine, have been "youthful prodigies." A schoolboy (let us say) who has just learned the moves, and has fallen under the chess-spell (the very names and shapes of the pieces are a sheer delight to him) sees a problem in some journal or other. It is improbable that he will find the correct solution, or, if he should do so, that he will realise what it is all about. But he will say to himself "Mate in two moves—I can make something like that." So he sends up a crudely-drawn diagram, the Key a capture and a check, with a single Black reply, and a triumphant mate. A kind chess editor will not abash the boy with a vitriolic pen, but will point out that Black should be given alternative defences, and will recommend an elementary text-book and the study of published positions. The tyro will then discover, with intense joy, the idea of variation play; not the long, dull variations of chess openings (I write from the point of view of the born problemist) ending in equality of position or an imperceptible advantage to one side, but a neat little box of tricks that finishes off White's contract on the stroke of time. Next, possibly, he will come across another novelty, the waiting Key. In the game, a *coup de repos* rarely occurs outside the "opposition" in pawn endings, when mate is still far ahead. The beginner loves, especially, to deliver mate, and will be fascinated by a Block position, that compels Black to choose one of several ways of immediate suicide. His second effort at composition may be something like this:—

Mate in 2

Composer's Key P = Kt, waiting

A young problemist is almost certain to rediscover the ancient, threadbare device of a Kt promotion Key. The marvel that Black can be allowed to check his enemy, just before his own doom (discovered from a problem he has solved) has made a strong impression, and he has thoroughly enjoyed working three specimens into his diagram. It will be returned, to his sorrow, with the following comments. P = Kt has lost the merit (its only one) of surprise as a Key. The fact that a Black check (Kt × Q) has to be provided with a reply is a very bad feature; a solver will see this Black counter-attack almost at once, and will be led to the Key. There is little merit or interest in Black checks that are "set" in the diagram, especially when they are met by capture of the checking piece. The Key should introduce them, and they should, if made into a theme, be countered by the more subtle "Cross-Check." There is nothing to be gained by displaying, in the diagram, most of the White forces in an *en prise* position. The beginner is always too fond of sacrifices, which should be done by the Key, if at all, and should produce distinct mates. Sacrifices of White, if apparent before the Key, merely limit its possible range. The criticism of the boy's No. 2 will include the impossible position of Black's KB (he might at the same time learn the meaning of "obtrusive" force: see page 7) and the Cooks by Kt – B5 ch and Kt – B8 ch.

At this stage, the majority of beginners will become discouraged at the arduous prospect before them. School life does not encourage the Solitary, as the problemist must be, in his creative hours. Such boys would be known as "freaks" in my own school. Not many masters (or parents) encourage one of the purest of the minor arts. There is little money in playing chess, and practically none at all in composing chess problems. A very few lads will steadily develop their powers of construction, and of these a handful will become (usually in the early twenties) expert craftsmen. It is a curious thing, this business of making problems. The mathematical and the artistic faculties (for want of better adjectives) seem blended together, as they are in scarcely any other pursuit. To the looker-on, this crouching by oneself over a chessboard for hours at a stretch, continually shifting a few units of force, of different functions, along two dimensions, seems an inconceivable waste of time. To the composer, it seems that his brain is working at its highest tension, and producing its finest capabilities. As for the rest of his body, it has hardly a conscious existence, during those hours. When it *does* wake up and protest, it is time to put away the chessmen. I advise the composer to set himself a fixed duration for a particular day's work, and stick to it, however near he may think himself to his goal. He must have a stock of diagrams, on which he can keep records of alternative settings, as he goes along. Some composers deliberately put aside an unfinished diagram until they have half forgotten the setting. They return to it with a fresh outlook and the full use of their critical faculties, which tend to become dimmed by the intense business of composing. A variation that would not come out may yield to a new inspiration, or the composer may find that it is not so indispensable to his scheme as he thought. Or, again, he may discard a "star" line with a reluctance somewhat appeased by a new choice of options, in dealing with what is left of the play. The great composers usually have two standards of positions; first, those suitable for a Composing Tourney; and secondly, for casual publication. Their second strings are, of course, of considerable merit, but in some way (insufficient originality, it may be, or Duals, or slightness of total effect) they fall short of a high ideal.

The procedure of a problem-composing tourney is something like this. A journal makes an announcement, giving the date up to which entries can be made (usually about six months ahead), and offering prizes (three is an average number). The judge (or judges) is named. He should be, of course, a composer or connoisseur of repute, who takes a wide view of the art. A judge who is known to have prejudices will attract too many entries that suit his particular whims. It is most advisable for a composer's identity to be kept a secret; the judge must be protected against any suspicion of favouritism. A cumbersome method to achieve this end is the duplicate diagram process. The composer sends the editor two diagrams of his problem, one without his name, which is forwarded to the judge; the other, with his name added, is enclosed in a sealed envelope, and is kept by the editor, who opens it when the prize-award has been made. This method is troublesome and unsafe; for an expert may well recognise a composer's peculiar script in the solution (which must always be given) or even in his diagram. It is now usual for only one diagram of a problem to reach the editor, who copies it out, unnamed, for the judge's perusal. The judge will arrange the positions in his order of merit, and should certainly send all aspirants for honours to George Hume, the Curator of the A. C. White Collection, who will give them an expert examination for complete or partial anticipations. The judge will then be in a position to make his final award, which will generally add a number (up to a dozen) of problems to the prize-winners, for "honourable mention," and then "commendation."

The British Chess Magazine, in its problem pages conducted by B. G. Laws and T. R. Dawson, publishes the winning diagrams of all composing tourneys of importance. Writing in the middle of 1930, I find that the most successful Two-move tourney composers of the last two years have been J. A. Schiffmann (Roumania), C. Mansfield (England), A. Mari (Italy), L. A. Issaeff and S. S. Lewmann (both of Russia). A. Ellerman (Buenos Aires) and A. Bottacchi (Italy) seem to have recently dropped out of the fray.

I have said next to nothing about the actual machinery of composition. It is generally a case of trial by error until you get what you want, the expert having the great advantage over the novice of his quicker perception of a *cul de sac*. A few small "gadgets" will soon be picked up by experiment, such as the "control" of an unwanted White K in a Block. The most economical way is to place him on Kt1, with a Black B on R8 and a Black P on Kt7. The three units are neatly tucked up together, mere armchair-critics of the fray. This word, "control," is used a great deal by problemists, and I think it should be defined.

SQUARE CONTROL is guard of a particular square, so that a piece that occupies it can be captured. In effect, the square is *"en prise."* The expression applies equally to White control of squares that Black wants to occupy, or Black control of squares that White wants. Guard of a K flight is logically included.

PIECE CONTROL is the subjugation to the composer's wishes of a unit that he cannot omit. A great deal of it occurs in Block positions, where there is partial or complete paralysis of White or Black units, the former (usually) to prevent Cooks, and the latter to prevent "no solution." In Threat positions, also, one frequently finds a Black piece, some of whose moves make necessary variations, while others, not wanted by the composer, unkindly insist on defeating the threat. This piece has to be controlled by some means or other, generally by providing "fringe" variations, or plugging its recalcitrant squares. One of many examples in this book is shown in No. 43, where the Black QKt defeats the threat by any move. Most of its options are met by a series of devices (Black Interference, etc., that make up one of the themes) but Kt – Kt3 or Kt5 were not amenable, and Black P plugs had to be put on those squares, to complete the control.

Returning to the mechanism of composition, the following account of my own methods, in constructing a couple of rather poor problems, may help a little. It will show only a few of the salient ideas that occurred to me, and may be compared to the selection of one in a hundred (at a guess) of the photographs in a moving-picture.

SCENE: A large room in a Scarborough Hotel, in which a Chess Congress is proceeding. Victor Rush, cheeriest and most persuasive of chess enthusiasts, insists on my composing a problem for an editor-friend of his. Sitting down in a vacant chair (and state of mind) in this "Temple of Caissa" (as some misguided people would call it—I detest that stucco goddess, the alleged patron of chess, whose name was coined in the imitation-antique period of our literature) I juggle with a few pieces, until a small idea suggests itself. At this stage a kindly stranger comes along, and taking pity on my loneliness at the board offers me a game. I explain that I am engaged in the much more interesting business of composing a problem. Upon which he departs, wearing the compassionate look that one keeps for well-meaning but slightly imbecile acquaintances. I am reminded of my friend, G. W. Chandler's experience as a car-driver in Mespot. Guy Chandler is an excellent and enthusiastic problemist, but he detests the game of chess. As soon as ever he got going on a new composition, one of his mates, pitying the poor chap trying to play chess with himself, would come along and insist on an immediate contest. Chandler, boiling inwardly, felt constrained to conceal his mysterious hobby.

DIAGRAM A

IDEA: a Block-Threat. Key R – QB4. Threat R – B6, which will also follow 1. K – B2. If 1. Kt – B2, 2. B – B2, instead of the set 2. R – K6. This changed mate, and the flight-giving Key, make up the idea. We leave the method of controlling the other squares in the Black K field until more ideas arise and are dealt with, noticing that 1. P – Kt5 will be met by 2. R × P.

HOPE: that some further changed or interesting variation play will arise.

CRITICISM: the important K move should lead to a mate that is distinct from the threat. Otherwise, the flight-gift is a cheap affair.

INFERENCE: R – KKt4 should be the mate; so I take off the Black P.

INTERRUPTION: several excellent players, who are not problemists, inform me that the White K is not on the board. I thank them, put him on, and remove him, when they have passed beyond my ken.

IDEA: the Key will gain a distinct snap if the K flight should introduce a Black check, from a Q or R on the KKt file, which will be "crossed" by 2. R – KKt4.

INFERENCE: all the pieces must be moved one rank down-wards, when the White K goes upon KKt8, so as to allow the Black K to come out with discovered check.

CRITICISM: but now the Black Kt, in his Self-Block variation, delivers check, which I can't permit.

INFERENCE: some other Black unit must perform the Self-Block operation, and it must be one that will allow the set-mate. I give the board a quarter-turn, put on a Black P, and arrive at "B."

DIAGRAM B

Key R—B6. Threat R—K6.

If 1. P—B6, 2. B—R6 (instead of R—K4)
If 1. K—B6 ch, 2. R—B2

INTERRUPTION: further and better players (also non-problemists) tell me the board is wrongly placed. That KR1 must be a White square. I thank them and put it right. This is quicker than an explanation of the methods of the problemist, who saves time by giving half and quarter turns to the board instead of moving all the pieces.

CRITICISM: how is 1. P – B6 to prevent the threat, and force B – R6?

IDEA: the P might come from KKt5, capturing a White unit on B6, and opening a gate for a Black B on KR6. So we come to C.

DIAGRAM C

In C, a White P is added at KKt3, to prevent P – Kt6 check. It has a second use, in guarding a square when the Black K moves out. Naturally, I don't want a solver to realise this fact, and hope the prevention of the Black P check will account for the unit, in his opinion. A great point in a flight-giving Key is made, when the guard of the squares in the *extended* K's field can be completed, without providing sign-posts for the solver. A Black P on QR6 is also added in C, to prevent R × B in the B – R6 mate.

CRITICISM: there must be more variation play, and I turn my attention, first of all, to the pieces already on the board.

IDEA: try the Black R. Put him on QKt7, and a Black B on QR8, so that any move of the R will prevent the threat, by opening a gate for the B. These R moves must be controlled. 1. R – R7 is not promising, so I transfer the Black P (R6) to R7, to plug this square. 1. R – B7, or any move off the rank, will clearly allow 2. R – B2 mate. There is left 1. R – Q7, the only hope, but a promising one, for a new variation by this piece. A self-block suggests itself at once, and, by pushing the position one rank up, I get D. The diagram contains a new White piece (Kt on K1) which is released by the R self-block, and covers the flight-square in its mate on Kt2. Three other White units are added simply to control the Black K, and complete the scaffolding.

DIAGRAM D

Key R—B7. Threat R—K7

Black	White
I	2
K×P ch	R(B7)—B3
(R—B6, etc.)	
P×P	B—R7
R—Q6	Kt—Kt2

CRITICISM: there is still too little variety for the force employed. Also 1. R × Kt and 1. B × Kt both defeat the threat. The former could be prevented by a White P on QKt4 (a hateful breach of White economy), but the latter is not so easily met.

IDEA: Why not improve the Key by sacrificing a R (on KB4) to the Black K, instead of a mere P? This R would hold Q4 (when 1. R × Kt wouldn't matter) and could give a White Interference mate (a favourite device of mine) after the self-block 1. R – Q6, by adding a White B on KR7. The White Kt on K1 goes back to the box. To meet 1. B – B7, a further idea suggests a White Q on KKt2, both to capture this B and to replace the White R (B2) and B (R8). We get a new variation, and the substitution of the Q for R and B must be considered an economy. Diagram E, which follows, contains also a Black P on QB7, against the defence 1. B–Kt8.

DIAGRAM E

The new play is: 1. R – Q6, 2. R – K4, and 1. B – B7, 2. Q × B.

REVIEW: A fairly respectable set of variations has been put together, and I proceed to hunt for Cooks. The Key R is considered first. R – B6 (or B8) threatens mate on the K file, as the actual Key does. These Cooks are not too easily dealt with, considering that the threat line, from K7 to the Black K, must be inviolable. Moreover, R (B5) – B4 and R – Q5 are both nasty jars, one threatening B – R7, and the other R – K4.

SHOCK: suddenly I behold R – KB3, short mate! A Black Kt on KR7 stops this and makes yet another variation by 1. Kt – B6 or Kt × P, 2. R – KB3. A further Cook now appears by 1. R – K4 ch K – Q6, 2. Q – K2 or R – Q5.

SHOCK No. 2: I note, with more amusement than surprise, that the original idea of a Complete Block, set before the Key, has evaporated, almost from the start. All that is left is the changed mate, after 1. P × R, which has lost its relative importance. The problem has become, practically speaking, an ordinary Threat, with a good, if familiar sort of Key, and modest variety.

DIGRESSION: this is exactly what happens to the composer, in nine cases out of ten, unless he is working on a very clear-cut idea. His early variations gradually cease to be necessities in his eyes; they lose their importance, and are replaced by other schemes, and the final result is as far removed from the beginning as Z from A. I have sometimes found myself obsessed with a single variation, which would not, by any means, mingle nicely with other play; have worried myself almost to distraction over it; and then, becoming sensible, have calmly reviewed the position, and thrown the Jonah overboard, quite glad to get rid of him.

I do not propose to set down, even if I could present them in any kind of order, my struggles against the Cooks mentioned above. The final arrangement came out thus:

No. 160
B. Harley. Observer, August 1928

Mate in 2
Key R—B7. Threat R—K7

The variation in E, 1. B – B7 2. Q × B is replaced by 1. Kt – Kt6, 2. Q × Q, a Black Interference, and therefore superior in quality. Defences to various tries are 1. R – Q5, Q × Q; 1. QR – B4, P – K8; and if 1. R – K4 ch K – Q6, the unpinned Black Q prevents mate.

Final criticism: the machinery for making the problem sound is much too cumbrous. The White Q does very little for her importance, and the outlying White Kt on K8 (whose sole use is the prevention of a Cook by 1. R – B8) is a monstrosity. A White P, added for Cook-prevention, may occasionally pass muster, but anything larger is almost inexcusable, in modern opinion. I found it impossible to use one of the Black R's (on the KR file, say) to stop 2. R – K8, since both are wanted elsewhere. The R on Q8 prevents 1. P – Q8 (when there would be no solution) and this P seemed the only way to cover White's Q2. The problem ought, perhaps, to have remained in obscurity, but a fit of obstinacy (combined with a scarcity of originals at the time) induced me to publish it in my own column, where it did some damage to solvers' scores.

Meanwhile, Victor Rush and his friend had still to be satisfied. I came back to the original idea of a Block (abandoning any hope of changed play) and evolved F.

DIAGRAM F

Key R—Kt7, waiting

A hopelessly ugly affair. The mingled P's on the QR file make one shudder. The Black P on R3 prevents 1. Kt ch K – B6, 2. Q × P (R5). That on R4 prevents 1. QR – Kt4. That on R7 prevents Black's 1. R × Kt, while the White P on R4 blocks a Black P, and the White P on B5 stops Cooks by Q or R – B6. After failing to economise and lighten this version, I gave up the R Key (with its flight-gift) altogether, and came to positions like G.

DIAGRAM G

Key Kt—Kt2, waiting

Black	*White*
1	2
K × R ch R—Kt8 or R × P }	R—Kt1
R—B8	R—Q2
P × R P × Kt }	Q—R4
Kt any	R—Q5

The Key introduces the Black check, but has to provide for 1. P × R and 1. R – B8. I dislike provision for such a strong-looking defence as 1. P × R, and abandoned this version. Finally, I had to be satisfied with the next diagram.

No. 161

B. Harley. Weekly Scotsman, Aug. 1928

Mate in 2

Key B—Kt4, waiting

The Key simply holds the mating-net. This is the only specimen I have ever produced of the old-fashioned Key that merely waits, without introducing new play. As such, in its rustic simplicity and smug satisfaction in the existing state of affairs, it tickled my fancy; for we composers must give way to our whims, at times. My friend, E. H. Shaw, an expert chess-player and problemist, uttered the best possible criticism of this composition: "What's it all about? What's it *for?*" What, indeed! Let me refer back to my fourth qualification for great composing, luck. That's it, of course. I was unlucky.

CHAPTER XI

SOLVING AND ANALYSING

1. *Solving in Competitions*

The serious business of solving in a competition demands not only technical knowledge, but also a thorough examination for flaws. In the case of a Two-mover, it is usual for the conductor of a solving tourney to require all Keys (i.e. the composer's intention and Cooks) or, alternatively, a claim of "no solution." He may add to his solvers' task a complete list of the variation play, including Duals, etc., and he may ask for a technical criticism.

Entrants in these competitions must take them seriously. Some conductors lay deliberate traps with cooked or unsolvable problems, and in this category they may place impossible positions, demanding a claim to that effect. Conditions should be adopted to the particular class of solvers who are likely to enter. What will suit the expert, almost professional solver, will not do for the "man in the café," who does not understand Duals and cannot be troubled to write down a string of variations. I have found the "Key or no solution" system quite adaptable for Two-movers in a popular journal. In a continuous series of solving tourneys, spread over eleven years, I have received some 80,000 solutions of 400 Two-movers, from 3,500 different entrants. Of these problems, thirteen were cooked, and two had no solution. In only two cases was the flaw deliberate, when I conspired with both those famous navigators, Captain Cook and Captain Kidd. But do you think I could get nine out of ten of my solvers to believe this? Not on your life. They hate Cooks as much as the proverbial young married couples of the comic press, and although *they* may fail to find them, they cannot allow the innocence of the composer, or the chess editor. As a matter of fact, some of the greatest composers are extremely casual in testing the soundness of their own problems; and if the editor's blind-spot should happen to occur at the same "locus," the mischief is done. Recriminations, apologies (sometimes), and a decrease in the number of leaders in the tourney, is the result of such accidental "separators," as we call problems that accomplish what is, after all, the object of a competition: the winnowing-out of the skilful *and careful* solvers from the rest. I should add that I consider the deliberate retention of Cooks a perfectly justifiable device, and I cannot see that an entrant who has found the composer's solution (and presumably has enjoyed it) has "wasted his time," as he is wont to complain, because he has missed a banal second solution. But I agree with him that "no solution" positions should not be set, with malice intent. There are solvers who enjoy Cook-hunting, but hardly one that likes to be completely baffled. And what of the casual solver, a non-competitor, who has not even the reward (in marks) allotted to the claimant of no solution? He probably confines his future attention to the acrostics and cross-words, especially the latter.

Marking Systems

There are many varieties. Mine is to give 10 for the composer's Key, and 5 for each Cook. If I marked for variations, I should give 2 for each forced mate, which would have to be accompanied by all the Black moves that introduced it. Duals would be 2 apiece, Triples 3, and so on. An actual Key, with a false claim of another, would get the 10 marking less the Cook marking, 5 on balance. Two or more false claims would wipe out the true key-marking altogether. A false claim of a variation (or Dual) would lead to a deduction of one mark from the problem's maximum. It seems to me to be a harsh policy to give nothing at all, when there is a single false claim, as some editors do. My system, like any other, is a compromise, but has worked well enough, with only occasional grumbles from my band of solvers.

Now, for some traps that I have found to claim most victims.

(a) Cooks. Only a beginner will take a blatant aggression, such as a check, to be the composer's intention. He has not much notion of what a problem is about, and cheerfully disregards the large number of units in the diagram that, as far as his Key is concerned, are simply spectators of a bit of horseplay. The experienced solver realises at once that the composer has "dropped a brick," and will go on looking for the idea. The kind of Cook that may deceive him is one that introduces (or allows by waiting) the composer's main-play. Naturally, a Cook that yields interesting variations, quite outside the composer's scheme, will be the most tricky of all. But such are extremely rare accidents.

(b) Tries, just defeated by the position of the White K. I wonder how many scores of cards I have sent out to aggrieved claimants who missed this point. "Watch the White K" should be almost the chief slogan for the inexperienced solver. This piece is the composer's best ally for Cook-prevention. It has to be on the board, and, so far, is above suspicion; but many a Try is defeated by a Black check that it allows, or, more subtly, by a pin of a White unit.

(c) Tries defeated by Unpins of Black force. Not so frequent as (b), but dangerous enough to the unwary. In fact, all pinning and unpinning strategy is especially puzzling (I have found) to the novice.

(d) Tries that partake of the nature of the deceitful Cooks mentioned in (a). That is, they reproduce enough of the real strategy to satisfy the solver, while failing against one or two defences. Nearly all Complete Blocks, before the Key, will have a few such Tries, and, if the true solution should introduce changed play, the inexperienced solver is likely to fall.

The expert, however, expects changed play in any modern Two-move Block.

(e) Intricacy of position. On the average, a novice will find a lightweight Two-mover more easy than a complex heavyweight. There are fewer units and lines of play to watch. To the expert, every additional piece becomes a new signpost. And where the Key is a spectacular Gift, it will probably be the first he will examine (knowing the propensity of composers), while it will be almost the last that will burst upon the astounded novice. In this connection, I may refer the reader to my remarks on Difficulty of Solution on page 46.

2. *Desultory Solving*

Most composers take their solving thus, glancing at their rivals' work, to keep themselves up to date in the latest thematic developments, with an occasional mental note of admiration at some well-known difficulty neatly overcome, or of criticism at some breach of their own particular crotchets. They will rarely look further than the thematic content, with side glances at the manner in which the composer has avoided Duals in his main variations, and such technical points. Blatant Cooks will not be searched for by the composer-solver, nor will he often trouble himself to enter a Solving Tourney.

3. *Analysing*

Yet there are a few composers, as well as solvers, who love to analyse a fine problem to its last dregs. They enter into all the composer's difficulties, find how he avoided each particular snag, balance the reasons for and against every alternative arrangement of the units, and finally give a judicious verdict on the whole matter, including originality, relative or actual, in their considerations. This is a true path to knowledge of both the construction and the solving of chess problems, and I shall now adopt it (very much curtailed, of necessity) in an examination of a series of positions. I have got to pretend I know nothing about them, like the author of a detective yarn, who carries his hero-sleuth through a series of carefully planned adventures.

No. 162

E. Boswell. Svenska Dagbladet, 1928

Mate in 2

I look at the name first. The manner of the crime betrayed the touch of Professor Moriarty to Sherlock Holmes; in chess problems, on the contrary, the composer's identity tells us, more or less, what to expect. In this case, it is good artistry from a young Lancastrian. Now for the problem. The Key must be of the waiting kind, for the only possible threat (on the first rank) can yield no variety, and is smashed by P – Kt7. I see that 1. P – Q5 is provided with 2. Q – R1, so the Q has got to remain on this diagonal. Try Q – Kt7. This meets a second Black move, P – Kt7, by Q × KtP; but P – B6 is an effective reply. Try Q – R8, which *must* be correct.

Black	White	Strategy
1	2	
P—Kt7	K—Kt4	Self-Block
P—B6	K×P	Unguard
P—Q5	Q—R1	Open Gate

187

There is evidently no extra force, put on for Cook or Dual prevention. Examine alternative units. The Q works on a file and a diagonal, as no other single unit could. The White K does noble work in holding two flights and discovering two mates. The B guards QKt1. It could not be elsewhere, for Q – B6 ch would be a Cook. Keys by the K and B would be bad, cutting off flights. The Q remains. She must not be able to reach the first rank at once. Consider a Key from a square on the QR file. This would give away the idea of the discovered checks. The choice left is between her actual square, and QKt7 or B8. On B8, she would have to provide for all three Black moves, making the Key more evident. On Kt7, two of the moves are provided with mates, and one is changed by the Key, a good feature. Let me try to read Boswell's mind. . . . He probably preferred QB6 for two reasons: (a) he liked to leave Q – Kt7 as a Try (b) on QB6 the Q has a very slightly greater option. Both reasons indicate, with greater force, why the Q and B are not on KKt8 and KKt6, respectively.

Remarks: A jolly Miniature, based on the two White K discoveries, with the QP added to control the Q's choice of squares on the QR file. The three variations are good value for the units. Miniatures, in which the number of units is limited to seven, and Merediths, where they count from eight to twelve, are often artificially restricted. I should never hesitate to add extra units, if such positions could be definitely improved, without losing their lightweight character. This is by the way, with no special reference to No. 162, which could hardly be extended without losing its unity of play. An afterthought: why did not the composer use a White Kt on Q2, instead of the B? First, he would have to find another Key, for Kt × KtP ch would be a Cook. Secondly, the Kt would have no range, for Tries.

Ruth Lindsay. Observer, Nov. 1929

Mate in 2

The unknown name intrigues one, for I don't know of a dozen women who have made a passable problem. The Black K has no flights, and the White K cannot be checked —two things that I look for, almost first of all, in any problem. Ignorant of the composer, I glance at Cook-tries by Q checks. Nothing doing. Let me guess at the theme, if any. The concentration of Black force, K, R, two Kts and a P, upon his K5 cannot surely be an accident. I plump for Kt – K4, a multi-sacrifice plus a K flight. Threat Kt – Q6. (The Key must be a threat, with such non-committal moves as B – Kt2 at Black's disposal.)

Black	White	
1		**2**
K × Kt	Q × RP	Model Mate
R or P × Kt	Q—B7	Self-Block
QKt × Kt	Q—QB8	do.
KKt × Kt	Q—Kt4	do.

The theme is the familiar Self-Block by Sacrifice. What happens if 1. Kt – Kt2, defending the threat-square? Why, Q × QP, by Black Interference. Next, look for plausible

Cooks. No move of the Q can threaten mate. We are left with the Kt, and only Kt – K8 is a possible alternative, so as to hold the flight-square with the same threat as the actual one, Kt – Q6. R × Kt is an obvious crusher. No Cook, therefore. What about Duals? Blocks of the Black K field are often Dual producers; and I see that 1. Kt – K3 allows the option of the threat or Q × RP; a minor dual, as both mates are otherwise forced. Now for the units. The White K, Q and Kt have evident uses. The composer had to control Q4, K3, K5 and KB6, all in the Black K's present or prospective field. Could the arrangement of the White B and P be economised? You have also to consider, jointly, the necessary cover of Q5, KB3 and 4, plugged in the diagram by Black P's. After examination, bearing in mind the relative importance of White economy to Black, and the slight embellishment of the Model Mate, I can find no improvement. The White B controls three squares, and although the White P, outlying the K's present field, indicates the flight gift, it is scarcely worth while to crowd the position, to avoid its use. An alternative arrangement, this B on QKt2 (say), with the Black R on K6 and a Black P on Q6, would fail against 1. P – Q5, cutting off the B. You would have to have a White P on QB4, instead of the Black P on Q4, giving 1. B × Kt instead of P × Kt, but also letting in a second Dual after 1. B – Q4, while you still have an outlying White P. The Black P on KB6 not only plugs that square, but prevents his fellow moving, which would defeat the Key. The P's on the KR file are left for consideration. That on R2 stops a double threat (Kt – Q6 or Q – Kt6) which would ruin the entire problem. The one on R3 can have only one use, to stop a Dual after 1. P – R3, by the threat or Q – Kt6. Why bother to stop it? Well, it is a Major Dual; for Q – Kt6 is never forced in the solution, and it is extinguished by the smallest possible addition.

Remarks: Quite a nice problem, not highly original, but neatly put together. The Key is typical of the theme, variety respectable for the force employed, and both the Black Interference and Model Mate are attractive additions. The

Dual, and perhaps the two sets of doubled P's, are very slight objections. The outlying White P, a Key signpost, is a bad mark in a Flight-Gift Theme. I note that the Black B must be on QR1; otherwise, its move from the diagonal would introduce Duals; and that the Black R is fixed on K7, for on K6 it would spoil the model, and on K8 it would cost a unit, to stop R – KR8 ch.

No. 164

G. W. A. Easom. Evening Standard, 1930

Mate in 2

A skilful young British composer, with a fondness for Pin-mates. He avoids highly complex strategy, and achieves originality by his total effects, rather than by variations that are novel in themselves. The Black K has, at present, no outlet, while the White K appears to have no critical use. The White KR's position leads me to guess that the Black K will be let out on K3, when his KKt will be pinned, and a Pin-Mate will result. Therefore, I try the QKt (on KKt7) for the Key piece, and the double sacrifice on K6 is the most plausible square. However, before going further, I eliminate the only other non-capturing spot, K8, with the same

threat, Kt - B7 (the Key must be a threat).   Obviously
1. R × Kt, 2. No mate.   Now for the variations following
1. Kt – K6, noting that any move of the Black KKt stops
the threat, but also deprives Black of his flight.

Black	White	
1	2	
K×Kt	Q×Kt	Pin-Mate
B×Kt	Q—K4	Self-Block
Kt—B3	Q—Kt3	do.
Kt—B5	Q—R8	Open Gate and Self-Block
Kt—B2	Kt—B6	Open Gate and Black Inter-ference and Pin-Mate
Kt—Kt5	Kt×B	Black Interference

No Duals, I think.   B – Kt5 at first sight seems to allow
the option of the threat or Kt × B; but I see that Black's
QR now protects his B.   The Key is good and thematic,
giving the flight around which the strategy is grouped.   On
the face of it, Kt7 is the best taking-off square.   I examine
the White force.   The Q, KR and Key Kt are essentials.
The Kt on R7 yields a good variation, and holds a square
when the K moves out.   It justifies its existence, but I
regret a little that it outlies the K's diagram field.   The White
QR, with the Black Kt that it pins, is dubious.   I hope
this combination is not introduced just to make 2. Kt – B6 a
Pin-Mate.   Then I notice that (1) Kt – Q2 must be stopped;
the composer's general scheme could hardly yield a new
variation from this move, and any Black unit that plugged
the square must be pinned, or it would stop the threat.   It
may as well be a Kt, to produce another Pin-Mate.   (2)
R – B1, defeating the threat, would be awkward to parry
otherwise.   The White QR has, therefore, a second use.   The
White B protects his P.   This P is a pity.   Why cannot it be
removed, allowing the B to hold a couple of squares?   I
notice one Cook (if that were done) by Q – Kt5 ch K – Q5,
2. B – Kt2 or Q – B5.   I admit the White P.   Why is the B
on QR3?   Examine the options.   Most of them would interfere with the play, while KKt1, etc., would allow the cut-off

of the defence of the P by B – K6. A single square, QKt6, is left without much objection, but I slightly prefer the look of QR3. And now I see something else. The B's position in the diagram prevents a Dual (Q – R2 or Q – Kt3) after 1. Kt – B3. A possible arrangement is B on QKt6 and K on QR2. The Black force has mostly been accounted for by the variation play. Note the P plugs on Q6, KB6 and KKt3, to complete White's control of the Black Kt. The P's on the R file are evidently added to prevent Duals by moves of Black's KR (2. Threat or Kt × B). Many modern composers would prefer to leave in this Minor Dual (it is technically a single Dual) rather than add two Black units. The White K would then be safe from checks on Q1. Admit the P's, and the K is rather better placed on (say) KR1, where he gives a second use to the P on KR6.

Remarks: A good Key, with good variety. A little too much square-plugging for everyone's taste, but this seems to be inherent in the scheme.

No. 165
A. G. Stubbs. Observer, March 1920

Mate in 2

A veteran of the art. This is a Waiter, or I will eat my hat in a public restaurant. The Black KB, plugged on his K side, and one of the plugging P's itself plugged; the other

Black B, ambushed by the White R, and no other darky but a Royal one, tell me the tale. The Black K has two flights, and there is certainly going to be Battery work from the Q + Kt and B + Kt artillery. The White K is on the line of the Black KB. At once, I know that White's QB will move away and allow the Black B + P Battery to open up against his Majesty. The Key must be B – K3, waiting, the P on B2 controlling his destination.

Black	White	
1	2	
P—K3 ch	QKt—Q6	Cross-Check and Self-Block
P—K4 ch	KKt—Q6	do. do.
K—B5	Kt—K5	Direct Battery
K—K3	Kt—B5	Indirect Battery
B moves	Kt—Q2	Avoidance of White Interference

The first, second, third and fifth variations show Direct Battery Mates, aimed against the Black K. The White force is all accounted for. The use of the R (and the Black B that it controls) may be thought, at first, rather "fringy." The composer evidently wanted to add a fifth opening of the Batteries, and, after all, QB6 and QKt5 have to be protected somehow. The R is passed, not with Honours, but passed. I don't much care for the White P plugs, but how can they be avoided? The thematic Key is a necessity, to my mind, in a Black Check Theme, and that accounts for the soldier on KB2. His comrade on Kt5 blocks a Black P. I look at the Black P on Kt3, the only unit of that colour that surprises me. Why could it not go back to the box, with the White P promoted to Kt6? There would be at least one terrible Cook by Q – B5 ch.

Remarks: A smart little problem. The Key is easy to me, because it is so thematic. Pleasant variation play, with a point in the Avoidance of 2. Kt – Q6, after 1. B moves. Various Cook-Tries, and some natural ones, likely to deceive until the Cross-Check idea is noticed. A good point also is the set mate, Q – Q3, after 1. P – K3, changed by the Key ;

but I dislike the necessary provision for the other flight, to K3. Originality? *In toto*, I imagine, not in separate details. The discovered checks by one Black P, creating Self-Blocks, are popular devices.

No. 166 (HOWARD THEME)

C. Mansfield. Observer, October, 1925

Mate in 2

The general opinion, with which I concur, is that no greater Two-move composer than Comins Mansfield has existed. He carries on the classical tradition of the English School, into the wider path of modern composition, in a natural manner. His style is more restrained than that of the ultra-moderns, with infrequent touches of the bizarre.

The Key is a threat, since the Black BP can give away nothing, by its move. The Black K has a flight to Q4, not yet provided with a mate. The White Q, pinned by an immovable Black R, herself pins a Black Kt. The theme must be Unpin of the Q, which can be done only by the Black Kt Interferences on B6 and Kt6. Therefore, the Key unpins this Kt, and the Q must go to either Q3 or KB3, to allow both Unpins. Q3 must be my choice, providing for K – Q4 by 2. Kt – B7. The threat is seen to be P – Q5, only after the Key has been deduced from thematic considerations.

	Black	White
1	Kt—B6	2 Q—B5
	Kt—Kt6	Q—B4

Four variations only, but the composer has doubled the Howard Theme, no mean achievement. In this theme, the Key piece, itself pinned, unpins a Black unit, which in its turn unpins the Key piece. The White force accounts for itself, by the variation play and control of the Black K, except the P on Kt2. That, evidently, prevents P=Q from being a check, the White K being absolutely fixed, without alternatives, on KR3. This Black P, and his friend on Kt4, plug checks by the released Kt. The Black R on QR6 and P on QR5 stop a Cook by 1. B × R ch, the White Q's situation being as fixed as her K's. What I do *not* like, is the apparent escape of the Black K via Q4, which the Key must prevent. I think I have a bigger "complex" against provision for Black flights by the Key than most composers have; but I am sure Mansfield does not care much for it, and had to yield to stern necessity in this instance.

Remarks: A clever Task achievement. Not up to Tourney standard, but a good second-string.

No. 167 (SCHIFFMANN DEFENCE)
J. A. Schiffmann. Observer, September 1928

Mate in 2

Schiffmann is of Russian descent and lives in Roumania. These two countries are producing some of the most extraordinary artists of the problem-board. Schiffmann is the most brilliant star that I have seen since the rise of Ellerman, Guidelli and Mansfield, in both the quality and quantity of his work.

The Black K has two flights and there are two White Batteries, Q + Kt and B + Kt. I note that one flight, K – Q6, is set with 2. KKt – K5 mate, and the other, K – Q4, by 2. Kt – R5, shutting off the Black Q. Surely I have seen something like this, quite recently? Yes, Stubbs' No. 165, but the resemblance turns out to be a surface one. The theme lay in Black checks in that composition, so let us try K – B6 as the Key. If then R – B6 ch, we have a nice White Interference, 2. Kt – B4. But, unfortunately, this is not mate, for K × Kt; moreover, I must call myself an idiot for failing to see that the Key must be a threat (look at all the loose Black stuff!) and that K – B6 (or B7) threatens nothing. Anyhow, I have found that 1. R – B6 *must* defeat the threat, whatever it may be, for the White Interference mate cannot be an accident, or there is no justice in chess problems. The threat, then, is on the KB file, and, naturally, it must be by an opening of the Q + Kt Battery. It must also guard the Q4 flight; which marks the threat square as White's K7 (the Kt guards the flight alternatively from KB4 after 1. R – B6). So the QR makes the Key, to give up its square to the threat piece. This R must continue to hold White's KP, or there would be no mate after 1. K – Q4. Therefore the Key is QR – K8, with the threat, KKt – K7.

Black	White	
1	2	
K—Q4	Kt—R5	Shut-Off
K—Q6	KKt—K5	
R—B6	Kt—B4	White Interference
Q—Q4	KKt—K5	Self-Block and Shut-Off
Q×P	Kt—Kt4	Schiffmann Defence

All the mates are by Direct Battery opening. The Star variation is the last. In the Schiffmann Defence, a Black unit so pins itself that the threat move would unpin it, and so fail. Q × P self-pins the Q, which would be unpinned by 2. KKt – K7, and would be able to interpose. It is therefore an Avoidance Theme. Now I notice a little ornament, added by the Key, in 1. Q – R2 ch, which actually adds nothing new, but pleases, as it costs no extra force. And, I see that in the variation list given above, KKt – K5 appears twice as a mate. This is a fair example of two distinct variations ending in the same mate, with which No. 156 may be compared. After 1. K – Q6, the particular Kt's move is compelled, in order to hold QB4. After 1. Q – Q4, on the other hand, it must go to K5 to shut off interposal by the Q.

Now, for the units of force. All the White pieces have evident uses in the play except the P on Q6. This, I see, stops a Cook by 1. KKt – K5 ch K – Q4, 2. R – Q8 mate. The K's position is fixed by the snap effect of the Cross-Check line introduced by the Key. The KB must be *en prise* to the Black Q. The QB might be on KB2, but it is rather better on Kt 1, for open effect, and this also is the argument for the place of the KR, which would make a crowd on KB6. The Black K, Q, and R are fixtures (the R cannot be on Kt6, for R × B would kill the Key). Consider the P's. QB6, Q7 and K7 are necessary blocks for 1. K – Q6. KKt4 has two functions; it stops a Cook by R – B4 ch, and a "no solution" by the pin 1. R – Kt6. The P on QKt7 puzzles me. Its only use can be to prevent 1. Q – B7, introducing a Triple by 2. Threat, Kt – Kt4, or QKt – K5; and 1. Q – Kt7, with a Dual. But Q – Kt8, with the Triple following, remains. Such *partial* remedies of the same Triple are hardly worth extra force, to my mind. I should prefer either to leave them all in, or to complete the process by adding a Black B on QKt8. Dr. Schiffmann's treatment of Duals seems rather old-fashioned, and contrasts with every other phase of his work.

Just as I have written these words (in the middle of last June) comes a letter from Comins Mansfield, telling me of the premature death at the age of twenty-six of this great composer, whose problems have been only five years before the public. F. F. L. Alexander and myself, as joint judges, have recently awarded Schiffmann first prize in a Two-move Composing Tourney of the British Chess Problem Society (Diagram No. 169 of this book) and I hope my friend and correspondent knew of this honour, before he put down his King.

Remarks on No. 167 above: The Schiffmann Defence is necessarily expensive in White material (see the White KP and QR, which enter only into the thematic variation) and one must bear this in mind in any criticism of the force-economy. The Key is absolutely thematic, as it should be, in an idea that depends on a single variation. The composer has graced his problem with two flights and good subordinate play by 1. Q – Q4 and 1. R – B6.

No. 168

C. G. Watney. Observer, October 1930

Mate in 2

Charles Watney acquired his finished technique in the early twenties, both of the century and of his age. Alain C. White has christened him "The Great Economist," because of the extraordinary complex results he obtains from a few pieces. Watney shows welcome signs of returning to the art that he had abandoned in 1925. Thenabouts, he told me he never intended to compose again, and I smiled up my sleeve.

The Black K has a flight, set with either Kt – K7 for the mate. The variation is trite and unthematic, and I know that Watney, very much of a modern, pays the slightest regard to Duals. The flight will doubtless enhance the real theme, whatever it may be, but its variation is not important. The general grouping of the White pieces, in particular the two R lines up against the Black K, coupled with the position of the Kts, suggests very strongly that White Interference is the theme. I see, right away, that Kt × P allows a fine specimen, by QKt – K7. This is a combination of White Interference by Self-Block (on K5) and Open Gate (K6, now held by the White KB). Next, any other move of this Kt allows the thematic mate, by Open Gate only, by KKt – K7. The natural conclusion is that the Key blocks the position. The Key piece is undoubtedly the Q, who is a mere spectator in the diagram. I see, next, that the Black KKt wants to go to K5 (or rather the composer wants him to go there; poor old Black would rather not move, please, in any problem), to introduce a third White Interference by Kt – Q4. So I conclude that the Key is Q – KKt1, holding Kt4 and Kt6 in this variation. This is confirmed by the mate following B – Kt3, Q – B2, while B – R7 is supplied for any other move of the Black B.

Black	White	
1	2	
Kt×P	QKt—K7	White Interference by Open Gate and Self-Block
QKt else	KKt—K7	White Interference by Open Gate
Kt—K7	Kt—K3	do. do. do.
Kt—B8	R—B4	do. do. do.
Kt—K5	Kt—Q4	White Interference by Self-Block with Open Gate Accessories
B—Kt3	Q—B2	Self-Block
B else	B—R7	Unguard

Duals after K – Kt3 and Kt – R8. There is only one unit that takes no part in the play, the Black P. This evidently stops Cooks by Q – QKt1 or B2 ch. The Great Economist has economised to some purpose.

Remarks: The Key is a routine one, completing the Block. Otherwise, a splendid achievement; five White Interferences, all accompanied by Open Gate effects, and with a flight square. The 1. Kt – K5, 2. Kt – Q4 variation has not the full thematic content of the other four White Interferences. There is not identity, here, of the square shut off by the mating unit (K4) and the opened up square (KKt4). Therefore, I call the Open Gate, as you will see above, an accessory in this case, and not a correlated feature. On this point of the correlated square, Watney queried a variation in No. 87. He maintained that the variation 1. Q – K5 was not a true example. The Black Q opens the White QB upon the critical square Q4, but (said Watney) it is she who shuts off the R from this square, and not the mating P. Well, I maintain that, in the mate, the P *does* shut off his R, and the fact that it replaces a Black unit does not invalidate the strategic combination. I asked Watney this pertinent question: Does the variation 1. Q – B5 2. Kt × Q (by his argument, no true thematic White Interference by Open Gate) differ essentially from 1. Q × P 2. Kt – B4? I cannot see that it does. Whether the Q chooses to sacrifice herself on the critical line, or no, seems to me immaterial. In No. 168, however, there is, *in the actual mate*, a Black Kt intervening on the critical line. Andrade more or less agreed, but would prefer the mate to be a non-capture. He calls the variation a special case, one of a dozen such in the Open-Gate-White-Interference Theme. I suggested he should write a book, with a chapter on each case! And he could, too. Barry Andrade exists only for the sake of the chess problem, of which he is, I suppose, the most versatile living exponent. It is a wonderful experience to hear him, in the luncheon hour of the Gambit Restaurant, pouring forth the whole of the problem art to a stranger, up for the day from the country, for a quiet game of chess. Watch the victim's growing terror and embarrassment, as Andrade gets more and more technical, his fingers setting up positions, one after the other, with inconceivable rapidity.

And such queries as this are hurled at the poor man, who has never even heard of a chess problem before: "Now, here is a Lateral Anti-Bristol, with a two-spot Diagonal Wurzburg Plachutta. Do you think that a third spot could be worked in? Or don't you?"

No. 169

J. A. Schiffmann. British Chess Problem Society, 1930

Mate in 2

The Black K has no flight. The White K seems to have no critical use. The theme evidently lies in the opening of the two White R + Kt Batteries.

At present, the Battery on the Q file is spiked by Q × R. That on the rank is twice defended, by both Q and R. The R can be shut-off by Kt – Kt5, but the Q's focus of both White R's remains. Let me make a Cook-Try, 1. QKt any ch, Q × QR; and now the other Battery is paralysed, for QB3 must be held, and the QKt is also paralysed, to hold Q5. Let me try the other Kt. Evidently Q × R must be the defence, for R – Kt5 will yield 2. R × R mate. But here again, the alternative Battery cannot open for mate, nor can the KKt find a mating square, QKt3, K2, K6, and KB3 being all defended. In solving this series of problems, I have not gone much into the question of Cook-Tries (which assumes unsoundness for the moment), but in this example my attempts have helped me to understand the limitations of the Batteries, and have accounted for a good deal of the Black force. Now, what is the Key, which must be a threat, and must keep the Batteries intact? I look at R – Q6 or 7, and see Q – QR1 or Kt1 ch, which tells me why the White K is so placed. Next, R – B4, defeated by R – Kt5. Again, Q × P or P – K6, threatening a diagonal mate with the lady. No good against R – Kt3. Again, Q – B4, met by R – Kt5. Not one of these tries would be such a Key as one expects from Schiffmann. There is one possible threat left, which has the seal of the expert upon it: B – K8, threatening Kt – K3, and giving two flights to the Black K.

Black	White	
1	2	
K—B5	Kt × QP	
K—Q6	KKt—B3	
P—B 5	Kt—Kt4	Self-Block and Shut-Off
Q × B or Q—B1	Kt—Kt5	Shut Off

Dual after Q – Kt1 by 2. Threat or Kt – Kt5. White units to be accounted for are the P's on Kt6, K5 and KKt3. The first prevents a Dual threat, Kt – K3 or Kt6. The second, two Cooks by 1. Kt – Kt4 ch Q × R, 2. Q × QBP, and by 1. Q × P mate (a "short" Cook). The third, a Dual after 1. K – Q6 by 2. KKt – B3 or Kt3. The Black Kt, the P's on QR5 and KB2, all stop Cooks by different moves of the White KKt, the last having a second use in its protection of the White K. The P on Q7 blocks his K, after 1. K – Q6. The P on KB3 stops 1. P – B3, fatal against the threat, even without the check to the White K.

Remarks: A magnificent study of White Battery play. The superb Key introduces a third Battery, Q + Kt, with direct or indirect use in three variations. A curious point arose in a discussion of this problem by Alexander, Andrade, Shaw, and myself, at the "Gambit." Why did Schiffmann use a Black Q, when, as it appears, a R would do as well? By careful testing, we found that the R would stop all Cooks, just as well as the Q, and the conclusion forced on us was that the R was rejected because it would create a Dual on *two* squares, KB1 or Kt1, against the Q's single Dual on Kt1. Schiffmann's lessening of the effect of the flaw by magnification of the R is typical of him, and my remarks on the Dual in No. 167 apply here. One other, a more important point, was mooted. Could not a mate by Kt – Kt6 be worked in, making six openings of the Batteries? Knowing well the composer's skill, we were sure he had tried it. Why then did he reject the position given below?

No. 169A

Mate in 2

Key B – K8. Threat Kt – K3

The added variation is 1. B × P 2. Kt × B.

Here are some objections that probably occurred to Schiffmann. Foremost, the Black P on Kt6 (it stops Q – Kt6, etc., destroying the threat). This P puts a second cover on a square after 1. K – B5 2. Kt × QP. Therefore it slightly lessens the surprise of the flight-gift by the Key. On the other hand, a neat Avoidance of 2. Kt – Q6, a White Interference, is introduced. Secondly, the Dual by 1. R – KKt1, mentioned above. Also, the composer was not necessarily trying for a great number of Battery openings (six is nowhere near a record). The Kt × B mate, being a symmetrical echo of the threat, is not worth so much as the other mates, which are introduced by more distinct Black strategy. And yet, we four composer-critics were fairly decided that this additional mate was worth while. There may have been other and more subtle objections in Schiffmann's mind. We shall never know.

CHAPTER XII

NEW DEVELOPMENTS

Before coming to the main subject, a few comments on the former edition will be useful.

(1) Errors are corrected with (I hope) only one exception. Diagram No. 7, a mere study, has no mate after 1. K – B6 P – Kt5. It is not only impossible but also insoluble !

(2) B. J. de C. Andrade has produced *five* specimens of Pin-models (see No. 96), but the key of his problem is a poor one.

(3) The Larsen Theme (No. 105) has since been done, and more than once, without *double*-check mate in the thematic line.

(4) The British Chess Problem Society (page 7) carries on bravely under its President, T. R. Dawson, who took over the post and sole editorship of the problem pages of the *British Chess Magazine* on the death of B. G. Laws in 1931. Among its numerous activities the Society represents this country in International composing and solving contests ; Great Britain won the last (1938) solving tourney, the problems being set by Austria, the winning country in 1937. The Society's organ, *The Problemist*, is conducted by C. S. Kipping, who is also Problem Editor of the magazine, *Chess*, and controller of the A. C. White Collection, since the death of George Hume in 1936.

BLACK CORRECTION

I give this name to a theme which has become very popular since my thesis on the subject, read before the B.C.P.S. in November, 1935. The theme (idea or motif, as some prefer to call it) lies in the analysis of difficult moves by the same Black unit. The player of Black (personifying him, as in a game) may find, on considering the alternative moves of one of his pieces, that non-defensive moves will allow a particular mate. Looking deeper, he sees that a special move (or it may be moves) by this piece will defeat that mate. Thus, he is able to correct the general error of moving the piece at random; the mate which (by the problem contract) must follow his Correction is different from the one allowed by the general error. A simple example will make this clear. Turn to No. 52. After the waiting key R – B8, assume that Black brings his R under consideration. It is evident that a random choice allows 2. B – K4 mate. He can, however, defeat this mate by R – Q5, when a Self-Block introduces 2. Kt – B3 mate. We can tabulate the mental processes of the problem-players thus:

(a) General Error: Line-Opening for the White B.
(b) Correction: Guard of White's K4.
(c) Final Error: Self-Block of White's Q4.

Black Correction (short for Black Self-Correction) should be clean-cut in all its phases, to be effective. In No. 52 the Black moves Kt – B4 and Kt – Q5 actually *maintain* the original defensive purpose of this piece—prevention of R – R5 mate—and can scarcely be deemed to correct the general error of moving it. At most, we may say there is "Semi-Correction."

Here is another example of the Theme, in a threat-problem; in this type more interesting complications of "B.C." can usually be shown.

No. 170 BLACK CORRECTION
S. Ceder.   First Prize British Chess Federation Tourney, 1939.

Mate in 2

Key Kt—Kt6

Threat Q × P(B4)

Black	White
1	2
Kt—Q2	Q × Kt
Kt—B5	B—B6
QKt else	B—Q3
Kt—K6	Kt— B2
Kt—Q3	QR × Kt
KKt else	R—Q4

Each Black Kt makes two corrections. The General Defence (a preliminary process against a threat) made by the QKt moves is Line Opening for the Black KB; the General Error is unguard of White's Q3; the Final Errors are interferences of the Black Q and QB, respectively. In the case of the Black KKt the General Defence is pin of the White Q; the General Error is unguard of Q4; the Final Errors are Self-Block and Interference of the Black KB, respectively.

The name "Black Correction" has been criticised. Dawson, for instance, likes "Compensation" (or "Compensating Effects"), preferring the chess problem to be "lifted out of the conception of a mere contest into its proper geometrical atmosphere." I prefer the human aspect; as I wrote in the *Australasian Chess Review*, Black may be compared to a man who struggles against the adversities of this life, covering his mistakes, when he recognises them, as best he can, but doomed (as he knows) to eventual extinction. A foreign editor wished to call B.C. the "Mari Theme," that composer having produced a specimen in 1922, but the idea goes back at least as far as Sam Loyd in 1859. Dawson was rather severe on this point in the *British Chess Magazine*, provoking a reply published in English, from which I quote verbatim an extract: "In this case any conjecture about the mental condition of whom does such things, completely presposterously, may let his friends seriously preoccupied." However, all ended quite amicably.

DUAL STOPPING

The name would make an old-timer gasp, for the prevention of optional White replies to a specific Black move would be merely a matter of routine to him. However, some of the advanced moderns deliberately introduce duals, *or the idea of duals*, in order to show how Black can stop them. I use the word here in its general sense, covering duals, triples, quadruples, etc.

No. 171 DUAL STOPPING

I. Ebben.   First Prize, Maasbode Tourney, 1939.

Mate in 2

Key Q—B2. Six Threats

Black	White
1	**2**
Q×B	Kt—B4
Kt×B	Q—Q4
Kt—B6	Q×Q
P—B6	B×Q
R×Kt	Kt—K1
R or B×B	
or P—K6	Q—K3

Six threats, and not a single dual—sheer diabolism ! This sort of thing is unusual, and we more often find Dual Stopping on the lines of the Black QKt's moves in No. 46, where four of his moves allow the dual mates Kt – Kt5 or B4.   Mansfield was, of course, only interested in the cross-check variations. Recent work has developed the idea, introducing more than one Black unit, each of which permits duals, triples, etc. (the

No. 172 DUAL STOPPING

F. Storm.   British Chess Magazine, March, 1940.

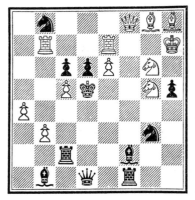

Mate in 2

Key KR—QB7

Threat Q×P

Black	White
1	**2**
1. R×P	P—K7
1. B×P	Kt—K7
1. P×P	Kt—B4

more choices the better, thematically) by non-defensive play, while special moves force distinct mates. The theme has other and stranger aspects: instead of a Black piece as the protagonist, a square (or a line) may be thematised.

In No. 172 the thematic square is that on which the White QBP stands. Black can capture this P, self-blocking the square, in three ways, preventing the *inherent* triple mate by various devices. Dawson tells me that he is approaching the view that there *ought* to be a dual in Dual Stopping themes, to underline the idea; (he may agree with me that it is not necessary in the case of a dual threat, when White clearly proclaims his dual intentions). In No. 172, a Black R could be added on QKt4 (with a Black P on QKt5, to prevent R×KtP). Then, if 1. This R×P, the triple mate follows. I do not maintain that the composer should have made such an ugly addendum, but that it could be even considered proves in what strange directions some of us are moving—the insertion of extra force *to allow a dual!*

WHITE HALF-PIN

This theme shows, on the analogy of the old (Black) Half-Pin Theme, the alternate pinning of two White

No. 173 WHITE HALF-PIN DIRECT
B. J. de C. Andrade.   Observer, January, 1940.

Mate in 2

Key R—B3

Thematic Tries

White	Black
1	1
KR×P, etc.	Kt—K5 !
B—B3	P×R !

units situated on the same line as their K. It is a Key-Theme, the interest lying in tries by these units. There are two main branches, Direct and Deferred.

The actual play can be worked out by the reader; the problem happens to be a Mutate, with a changed mate after 1. QKt any except – Q6. The point lies in the tries by the R on B4, leaving the White B pinned, and by the same B, leaving the R pinned.

No. 174 WHITE HALF-PIN DEFERRED

J. Bunting. Bristol Times, 1932.

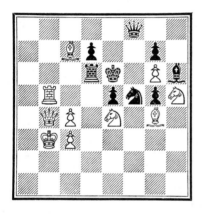

Mate in 2

Key KKt—Kt3

Thematic Tries

White	Black
1	1
R—R5	Q—QKt1 !
Q—R3	R—Kt3 !

Also, as it happens, a Mutate, with a changed mate after the Self-Block 1. Q—K2. Here, it will be seen, the White Q and R are not half-pinned in the diagram (as are the R and B in No. 173). The pinning defences by the Black R and Q are deferred until after the thematic tries. Andrade in particular has done much fine work on the theme, combining it (for instance) with a Black Half-Pin theme—a striking example of what it is now the fashion to call a "ditheme" (with "tritheme" for a medley of three themes). A specimen of this ditheme, by A. C. White and G. Hume, 1921, was actually the pioneer of the White Half-Pin theme.

INDEX OF NAMES

The numbers refer to the problem diagrams, except those in bold type, which are page references

GENERAL INDEX

Diagram numbers are printed in bold type

214

A CATALOGUE OF SELECTED DOVER BOOKS
IN ALL FIELDS OF INTEREST

A CATALOGUE OF SELECTED DOVER BOOKS
IN ALL FIELDS OF INTEREST

AMERICA'S OLD MASTERS, James T. Flexner. Four men emerged unexpectedly from provincial 18th century America to leadership in European art: Benjamin West, J. S. Copley, C. R. Peale, Gilbert Stuart. Brilliant coverage of lives and contributions. Revised, 1967 edition. 69 plates. 365pp. of text.

21806-6 Paperbound $3.00

FIRST FLOWERS OF OUR WILDERNESS: AMERICAN PAINTING, THE COLONIAL PERIOD, James T. Flexner. Painters, and regional painting traditions from earliest Colonial times up to the emergence of Copley, West and Peale Sr., Foster, Gustavus Hesselius, Feke, John Smibert and many anonymous painters in the primitive manner. Engaging presentation, with 162 illustrations. xxii + 368pp.

22180-6 Paperbound $3.50

THE LIGHT OF DISTANT SKIES: AMERICAN PAINTING, 1760-1835, James T. Flexner. The great generation of early American painters goes to Europe to learn and to teach: West, Copley, Gilbert Stuart and others. Allston, Trumbull, Morse; also contemporary American painters—primitives, derivatives, academics—who remained in America. 102 illustrations. xiii + 306pp. 22179-2 Paperbound $3.00

A HISTORY OF THE RISE AND PROGRESS OF THE ARTS OF DESIGN IN THE UNITED STATES, William Dunlap. Much the richest mine of information on early American painters, sculptors, architects, engravers, miniaturists, etc. The only source of information for scores of artists, the major primary source for many others. Unabridged reprint of rare original 1834 edition, with new introduction by James T. Flexner, and 394 new illustrations. Edited by Rita Weiss. 6⅝ x 9⅝.

21695-0, 21696-9, 21697-7 Three volumes, Paperbound $13.50

EPOCHS OF CHINESE AND JAPANESE ART, Ernest F. Fenollosa. From primitive Chinese art to the 20th century, thorough history, explanation of every important art period and form, including Japanese woodcuts; main stress on China and Japan, but Tibet, Korea also included. Still unexcelled for its detailed, rich coverage of cultural background, aesthetic elements, diffusion studies, particularly of the historical period. 2nd, 1913 edition. 242 illustrations. lii + 439pp. of text.

20364-6, 20365-4 Two volumes, Paperbound $6.00

THE GENTLE ART OF MAKING ENEMIES, James A. M. Whistler. Greatest wit of his day deflates Oscar Wilde, Ruskin, Swinburne; strikes back at inane critics, exhibitions, art journalism; aesthetics of impressionist revolution in most striking form. Highly readable classic by great painter. Reproduction of edition designed by Whistler. Introduction by Alfred Werner. xxxvi + 334pp.

21875-9 Paperbound $2.50

VISUAL ILLUSIONS: THEIR CAUSES, CHARACTERISTICS, AND APPLICATIONS, Matthew Luckiesh. Thorough description and discussion of optical illusion, geometric and perspective, particularly; size and shape distortions, illusions of color, of motion; natural illusions; use of illusion in art and magic, industry, etc. Most useful today with op art, also for classical art. Scores of effects illustrated. Introduction by William H. Ittleson. 100 illustrations. xxi + 252pp.

21530-X Paperbound $2.00

A HANDBOOK OF ANATOMY FOR ART STUDENTS, Arthur Thomson. Thorough, virtually exhaustive coverage of skeletal structure, musculature, etc. Full text, supplemented by anatomical diagrams and drawings and by photographs of undraped figures. Unique in its comparison of male and female forms, pointing out differences of contour, texture, form. 211 figures, 40 drawings, 86 photographs. xx + 459pp. 5⅜ x 8⅜. 21163-0 Paperbound $3.50

150 MASTERPIECES OF DRAWING, Selected by Anthony Toney. Full page reproductions of drawings from the early 16th to the end of the 18th century, all beautifully reproduced: Rembrandt, Michelangelo, Dürer, Fragonard, Urs, Graf, Wouwerman, many others. First-rate browsing book, model book for artists. xviii + 150pp. 8⅜ x 11¼. 21032-4 Paperbound $2.50

THE LATER WORK OF AUBREY BEARDSLEY, Aubrey Beardsley. Exotic, erotic, ironic masterpieces in full maturity: Comedy Ballet, Venus and Tannhauser, Pierrot, Lysistrata, Rape of the Lock, Savoy material, Ali Baba, Volpone, etc. This material revolutionized the art world, and is still powerful, fresh, brilliant. With *The Early Work,* all Beardsley's finest work. 174 plates, 2 in color. xiv + 176pp. 8⅛ x 11. 21817-1 Paperbound $3.00

DRAWINGS OF REMBRANDT, Rembrandt van Rijn. Complete reproduction of fabulously rare edition by Lippmann and Hofstede de Groot, completely reedited, updated, improved by Prof. Seymour Slive, Fogg Museum. Portraits, Biblical sketches, landscapes, Oriental types, nudes, episodes from classical mythology—All Rembrandt's fertile genius. Also selection of drawings by his pupils and followers. "Stunning volumes," *Saturday Review.* 550 illustrations. lxxviii + 552pp. 9⅛ x 12¼. 21485-0, 21486-9 Two volumes, Paperbound $10.00

THE DISASTERS OF WAR, Francisco Goya. One of the masterpieces of Western civilization—83 etchings that record Goya's shattering, bitter reaction to the Napoleonic war that swept through Spain after the insurrection of 1808 and to war in general. Reprint of the first edition, with three additional plates from Boston's Museum of Fine Arts. All plates facsimile size. Introduction by Philip Hofer, Fogg Museum. v + 97pp. 9⅜ x 8¼. 21872-4 Paperbound $2.00

GRAPHIC WORKS OF ODILON REDON. Largest collection of Redon's graphic works ever assembled: 172 lithographs, 28 etchings and engravings, 9 drawings. These include some of his most famous works. All the plates from *Odilon Redon: oeuvre graphique complet,* plus additional plates. New introduction and caption translations by Alfred Werner. 209 illustrations. xxvii + 209pp. 9⅛ x 12¼. 21966-8 Paperbound $4.00

DESIGN BY ACCIDENT; A BOOK OF "ACCIDENTAL EFFECTS" FOR ARTISTS AND DESIGNERS, James F. O'Brien. Create your own unique, striking, imaginative effects by "controlled accident" interaction of materials: paints and lacquers, oil and water based paints, splatter, crackling materials, shatter, similar items. Everything you do will be different; first book on this limitless art, so useful to both fine artist and commercial artist. Full instructions. 192 plates showing "accidents," 8 in color. viii + 215pp. 8⅜ x 11¼.   21942-9 Paperbound $3.50

THE BOOK OF SIGNS, Rudolf Koch. Famed German type designer draws 493 beautiful symbols: religious, mystical, alchemical, imperial, property marks, runes, etc. Remarkable fusion of traditional and modern. Good for suggestions of timelessness, smartness, modernity. Text. vi + 104pp. 6⅛ x 9¼.
20162-7 Paperbound $1.25

HISTORY OF INDIAN AND INDONESIAN ART, Ananda K. Coomaraswamy. An unabridged republication of one of the finest books by a great scholar in Eastern art. Rich in descriptive material, history, social backgrounds; Sunga reliefs, Rajput paintings, Gupta temples, Burmese frescoes, textiles, jewelry, sculpture, etc. 400 photos. viii + 423pp. 6⅜ x 9¾.   21436-2 Paperbound $4.00

PRIMITIVE ART, Franz Boas. America's foremost anthropologist surveys textiles, ceramics, woodcarving, basketry, metalwork, etc.; patterns, technology, creation of symbols, style origins. All areas of world, but very full on Northwest Coast Indians. More than 350 illustrations of baskets, boxes, totem poles, weapons, etc. 378 pp.
20025-6 Paperbound $3.00

THE GENTLEMAN AND CABINET MAKER'S DIRECTOR, Thomas Chippendale. Full reprint (third edition, 1762) of most influential furniture book of all time, by master cabinetmaker. 200 plates, illustrating chairs, sofas, mirrors, tables, cabinets, plus 24 photographs of surviving pieces. Biographical introduction by N. Bienenstock. vi + 249pp. 9⅞ x 12¾.   21601-2 Paperbound $4.00

AMERICAN ANTIQUE FURNITURE, Edgar G. Miller, Jr. The basic coverage of all American furniture before 1840. Individual chapters cover type of furniture—clocks, tables, sideboards, etc.—chronologically, with inexhaustible wealth of data. More than 2100 photographs, all identified, commented on. Essential to all early American collectors. Introduction by H. E. Keyes. vi + 1106pp. 7⅞ x 10¾.
21599-7, 21600-4 Two volumes, Paperbound $11.00

PENNSYLVANIA DUTCH AMERICAN FOLK ART, Henry J. Kauffman. 279 photos, 28 drawings of tulipware, Fraktur script, painted tinware, toys, flowered furniture, quilts, samplers, hex signs, house interiors, etc. Full descriptive text. Excellent for tourist, rewarding for designer, collector. Map. 146pp. 7⅞ x 10¾.
21205-X Paperbound $2.50

EARLY NEW ENGLAND GRAVESTONE RUBBINGS, Edmund V. Gillon, Jr. 43 photographs, 226 carefully reproduced rubbings show heavily symbolic, sometimes macabre early gravestones, up to early 19th century. Remarkable early American primitive art, occasionally strikingly beautiful; always powerful. Text. xxvi + 207pp. 8⅜ x 11¼.   21380-3 Paperbound $3.50

ALPHABETS AND ORNAMENTS, Ernst Lehner. Well-known pictorial source for decorative alphabets, script examples, cartouches, frames, decorative title pages, calligraphic initials, borders, similar material. 14th to 19th century, mostly European. Useful in almost any graphic arts designing, varied styles. 750 illustrations. 256pp. 7 x 10. 21905-4 Paperbound $4.00

PAINTING: A CREATIVE APPROACH, Norman Colquhoun. For the beginner simple guide provides an instructive approach to painting: major stumbling blocks for beginner; overcoming them, technical points; paints and pigments; oil painting; watercolor and other media and color. New section on "plastic" paints. Glossary. Formerly *Paint Your Own Pictures*. 221pp. 22000-1 Paperbound $1.75

THE ENJOYMENT AND USE OF COLOR, Walter Sargent. Explanation of the relations between colors themselves and between colors in nature and art, including hundreds of little-known facts about color values, intensities, effects of high and low illumination, complementary colors. Many practical hints for painters, references to great masters. 7 color plates, 29 illustrations. x + 274pp. 20944-X Paperbound $2.75

THE NOTEBOOKS OF LEONARDO DA VINCI, compiled and edited by Jean Paul Richter. 1566 extracts from original manuscripts reveal the full range of Leonardo's versatile genius: all his writings on painting, sculpture, architecture, anatomy, astronomy, geography, topography, physiology, mining, music, etc., in both Italian and English, with 186 plates of manuscript pages and more than 500 additional drawings. Includes studies for the Last Supper, the lost Sforza monument, and other works. Total of xlvii + 866pp. 7⅞ x 10¾. 22572-0, 22573-9 Two volumes, Paperbound $10.00

MONTGOMERY WARD CATALOGUE OF 1895. Tea gowns, yards of flannel and pillow-case lace, stereoscopes, books of gospel hymns, the New Improved Singer Sewing Machine, side saddles, milk skimmers, straight-edged razors, high-button shoes, spittoons, and on and on . . . listing some 25,000 items, practically all illustrated. Essential to the shoppers of the 1890's, it is our truest record of the spirit of the period. Unaltered reprint of Issue No. 57, Spring and Summer 1895. Introduction by Boris Emmet. Innumerable illustrations. xiii + 624pp. 8½ x 11⅝. 22377-9 Paperbound $6.95

THE CRYSTAL PALACE EXHIBITION ILLUSTRATED CATALOGUE (LONDON, 1851). One of the wonders of the modern world—the Crystal Palace Exhibition in which all the nations of the civilized world exhibited their achievements in the arts and sciences—presented in an equally important illustrated catalogue. More than 1700 items pictured with accompanying text—ceramics, textiles, cast-iron work, carpets, pianos, sleds, razors, wall-papers, billiard tables, beehives, silverware and hundreds of other artifacts—represent the focal point of Victorian culture in the Western World. Probably the largest collection of Victorian decorative art ever assembled— indispensable for antiquarians and designers. Unabridged republication of the Art-Journal Catalogue of the Great Exhibition of 1851, with all terminal essays. New introduction by John Gloag, F.S.A. xxxiv + 426pp. 9 x 12. 22503-8 Paperbound $4.50

A History of Costume, Carl Köhler. Definitive history, based on surviving pieces of clothing primarily, and paintings, statues, etc. secondarily. Highly readable text, supplemented by 594 illustrations of costumes of the ancient Mediterranean peoples, Greece and Rome, the Teutonic prehistoric period; costumes of the Middle Ages, Renaissance, Baroque, 18th and 19th centuries. Clear, measured patterns are provided for many clothing articles. Approach is practical throughout. Enlarged by Emma von Sichart. 464pp.   21030-8 Paperbound $3.50

Oriental Rugs, Antique and Modern, Walter A. Hawley. A complete and authoritative treatise on the Oriental rug—where they are made, by whom and how, designs and symbols, characteristics in detail of the six major groups, how to distinguish them and how to buy them. Detailed technical data is provided on periods, weaves, warps, wefts, textures, sides, ends and knots, although no technical background is required for an understanding. 11 color plates, 80 halftones, 4 maps. vi + 320pp. 6⅛ x 9⅛.   22366-3 Paperbound $5.00

Ten Books on Architecture, Vitruvius. By any standards the most important book on architecture ever written. Early Roman discussion of aesthetics of building, construction methods, orders, sites, and every other aspect of architecture has inspired, instructed architecture for about 2,000 years. Stands behind Palladio, Michelangelo, Bramante, Wren, countless others. Definitive Morris H. Morgan translation. 68 illustrations. xii + 331pp.   20645-9 Paperbound $3.50

The Four Books of Architecture, Andrea Palladio. Translated into every major Western European language in the two centuries following its publication in 1570, this has been one of the most influential books in the history of architecture. Complete reprint of the 1738 Isaac Ware edition. New introduction by Adolf Placzek, Columbia Univ. 216 plates. xxii + 110pp. of text. 9½ x 12¾.
21308-0 Clothbound $10.00

Sticks and Stones: A Study of American Architecture and Civilization, Lewis Mumford.One of the great classics of American cultural history. American architecture from the medieval-inspired earliest forms to the early 20th century; evolution of structure and style, and reciprocal influences on environment. 21 photographic illustrations. 238pp.   20202-X Paperbound $2.00

The American Builder's Companion, Asher Benjamin. The most widely used early 19th century architectural style and source book, for colonial up into Greek Revival periods. Extensive development of geometry of carpentering, construction of sashes, frames, doors, stairs; plans and elevations of domestic and other buildings. Hundreds of thousands of houses were built according to this book, now invaluable to historians, architects, restorers, etc. 1827 edition. 59 plates. 114pp. 7⅞ x 10¾.
22236-5 Paperbound $3.50

Dutch Houses in the Hudson Valley Before 1776, Helen Wilkinson Reynolds. The standard survey of the Dutch colonial house and outbuildings, with constructional features, decoration, and local history associated with individual homesteads. Introduction by Franklin D. Roosevelt. Map. 150 illustrations. 469pp. 6⅝ x 9¼.   21469-9 Paperbound $4.00

THE ARCHITECTURE OF COUNTRY HOUSES, Andrew J. Downing. Together with Vaux's *Villas and Cottages* this is the basic book for Hudson River Gothic architecture of the middle Victorian period. Full, sound discussions of general aspects of housing, architecture, style, decoration, furnishing, together with scores of detailed house plans, illustrations of specific buildings, accompanied by full text. Perhaps the most influential single American architectural book. 1850 edition. Introduction by J. Stewart Johnson. 321 figures, 34 architectural designs. xvi + 560pp.

22003-6 Paperbound $4.00

LOST EXAMPLES OF COLONIAL ARCHITECTURE, John Mead Howells. Full-page photographs of buildings that have disappeared or been so altered as to be denatured, including many designed by major early American architects. 245 plates. xvii + 248pp. 7⅞ x 10¾. 21143-6 Paperbound $3.50

DOMESTIC ARCHITECTURE OF THE AMERICAN COLONIES AND OF THE EARLY REPUBLIC, Fiske Kimball. Foremost architect and restorer of Williamsburg and Monticello covers nearly 200 homes between 1620-1825. Architectural details, construction, style features, special fixtures, floor plans, etc. Generally considered finest work in its area. 219 illustrations of houses, doorways, windows, capital mantels. xx + 314pp. 7⅞ x 10¾. 21743-4 Paperbound $4.00

EARLY AMERICAN ROOMS: 1650-1858, edited by Russell Hawes Kettell. Tour of 12 rooms, each representative of a different era in American history and each furnished, decorated, designed and occupied in the style of the era. 72 plans and elevations, 8-page color section, etc., show fabrics, wall papers, arrangements, etc. Full descriptive text. xvii + 200pp. of text. 8⅜ x 11¼.

21633-0 Paperbound $5.00

THE FITZWILLIAM VIRGINAL BOOK, edited by J. Fuller Maitland and W. B. Squire. Full modern printing of famous early 17th-century ms. volume of 300 works by Morley, Byrd, Bull, Gibbons, etc. For piano or other modern keyboard instrument; easy to read format. xxxvi + 938pp. 8⅜ x 11.

21068-5, 21069-3 Two volumes, Paperbound $10.00

KEYBOARD MUSIC, Johann Sebastian Bach. Bach Gesellschaft edition. A rich selection of Bach's masterpieces for the harpsichord: the six English Suites, six French Suites, the six Partitas (Clavierübung part I), the Goldberg Variations (Clavierübung part IV), the fifteen Two-Part Inventions and the fifteen Three-Part Sinfonias. Clearly reproduced on large sheets with ample margins; eminently playable. vi + 312pp. 8⅛ x 11. 22360-4 Paperbound $5.00

THE MUSIC OF BACH: AN INTRODUCTION, Charles Sanford Terry. A fine, nontechnical introduction to Bach's music, both instrumental and vocal. Covers organ music, chamber music, passion music, other types. Analyzes themes, developments, innovations. x + 114pp. 21075-8 Paperbound $1.25

BEETHOVEN AND HIS NINE SYMPHONIES, Sir George Grove. Noted British musicologist provides best history, analysis, commentary on symphonies. Very thorough, rigorously accurate; necessary to both advanced student and amateur music lover. 436 musical passages. vii + 407 pp. 20334-4 Paperbound $2.75

JOHANN SEBASTIAN BACH, Philipp Spitta. One of the great classics of musicology, this definitive analysis of Bach's music (and life) has never been surpassed. Lucid, nontechnical analyses of hundreds of pieces (30 pages devoted to St. Matthew Passion, 26 to B Minor Mass). Also includes major analysis of 18th-century music. 450 musical examples. 40-page musical supplement. Total of xx + 1799pp.
(EUK) 22278-0, 22279-9 Two volumes, Clothbound $17.50

MOZART AND HIS PIANO CONCERTOS, Cuthbert Girdlestone. The only full-length study of an important area of Mozart's creativity. Provides detailed analyses of all 23 concertos, traces inspirational sources. 417 musical examples. Second edition. 509pp.
(USO) 21271-8 Paperbound $3.50

THE PERFECT WAGNERITE: A COMMENTARY ON THE NIBLUNG'S RING, George Bernard Shaw. Brilliant and still relevant criticism in remarkable essays on Wagner's Ring cycle, Shaw's ideas on political and social ideology behind the plots, role of Leitmotifs, vocal requisites, etc. Prefaces. xxi + 136pp.
21707-8 Paperbound $1.50

DON GIOVANNI, W. A. Mozart. Complete libretto, modern English translation; biographies of composer and librettist; accounts of early performances and critical reaction. Lavishly illustrated. All the material you need to understand and appreciate this great work. Dover Opera Guide and Libretto Series; translated and introduced by Ellen Bleiler. 92 illustrations. 209pp.
21134-7 Paperbound $2.00

HIGH FIDELITY SYSTEMS: A LAYMAN'S GUIDE, Roy F. Allison. All the basic information you need for setting up your own audio system: high fidelity and stereo record players, tape records, F.M. Connections, adjusting tone arm, cartridge, checking needle alignment, positioning speakers, phasing speakers, adjusting hums, trouble-shooting, maintenance, and similar topics. Enlarged 1965 edition. More than 50 charts, diagrams, photos. iv + 91pp.
21514-8 Paperbound $1.25

REPRODUCTION OF SOUND, Edgar Villchur. Thorough coverage for laymen of high fidelity systems, reproducing systems in general, needles, amplifiers, preamps, loudspeakers, feedback, explaining physical background. "A rare talent for making technicalities vividly comprehensible," R. Darrell, *High Fidelity*. 69 figures. iv + 92pp.
21515-6 Paperbound $1.25

HEAR ME TALKIN' TO YA: THE STORY OF JAZZ AS TOLD BY THE MEN WHO MADE IT, Nat Shapiro and Nat Hentoff. Louis Armstrong, Fats Waller, Jo Jones, Clarence Williams, Billy Holiday, Duke Ellington, Jelly Roll Morton and dozens of other jazz greats tell how it was in Chicago's South Side, New Orleans, depression Harlem and the modern West Coast as jazz was born and grew. xvi + 429pp.
21726-4 Paperbound $2.50

FABLES OF AESOP, translated by Sir Roger L'Estrange. A reproduction of the very rare 1931 Paris edition; a selection of the most interesting fables, together with 50 imaginative drawings by Alexander Calder. v + 128pp. 6½x9¼.
21780-9 Paperbound $1.50

AGAINST THE GRAIN (A REBOURS), Joris K. Huysmans. Filled with weird images, evidences of a bizarre imagination, exotic experiments with hallucinatory drugs, rich tastes and smells and the diversions of its sybarite hero Duc Jean des Esseintes, this classic novel pushed 19th-century literary decadence to its limits. Full unabridged edition. Do not confuse this with abridged editions generally sold. Introduction by Havelock Ellis. xlix + 206pp.   22190-3 Paperbound $2.00

VARIORUM SHAKESPEARE: HAMLET. Edited by Horace H. Furness; a landmark of American scholarship. Exhaustive footnotes and appendices treat all doubtful words and phrases, as well as suggested critical emendations throughout the play's history. First volume contains editor's own text, collated with all Quartos and Folios. Second volume contains full first Quarto, translations of Shakespeare's sources (Belleforest, and Saxo Grammaticus), Der Bestrafte Brudermord, and many essays on critical and historical points of interest by major authorities of past and present. Includes details of staging and costuming over the years. By far the best edition available for serious students of Shakespeare. Total of xx + 905pp.
21004-9, 21005-7, 2 volumes, Paperbound $7.00

A LIFE OF WILLIAM SHAKESPEARE, Sir Sidney Lee. This is the standard life of Shakespeare, summarizing everything known about Shakespeare and his plays. Incredibly rich in material, broad in coverage, clear and judicious, it has served thousands as the best introduction to Shakespeare. 1931 edition. 9 plates. xxix + 792pp.   (USO) 21967-4 Paperbound $3.75

MASTERS OF THE DRAMA, John Gassner. Most comprehensive history of the drama in print, covering every tradition from Greeks to modern Europe and America, including India, Far East, etc. Covers more than 800 dramatists, 2000 plays, with biographical material, plot summaries, theatre history, criticism, etc. "Best of its kind in English," *New Republic*. 77 illustrations. xxii + 890pp.
20100-7 Clothbound $8.50

THE EVOLUTION OF THE ENGLISH LANGUAGE, George McKnight. The growth of English, from the 14th century to the present. Unusual, non-technical account presents basic information in very interesting form: sound shifts, change in grammar and syntax, vocabulary growth, similar topics. Abundantly illustrated with quotations. Formerly *Modern English in the Making*. xii + 590pp.
21932-1 Paperbound $3.50

AN ETYMOLOGICAL DICTIONARY OF MODERN ENGLISH, Ernest Weekley. Fullest, richest work of its sort, by foremost British lexicographer. Detailed word histories, including many colloquial and archaic words; extensive quotations. Do not confuse this with the Concise Etymological Dictionary, which is much abridged. Total of xxvii + 830pp. 6½ x 9¼.
21873-2, 21874-0 Two volumes, Paperbound $6.00

FLATLAND: A ROMANCE OF MANY DIMENSIONS, E. A. Abbott. Classic of science-fiction explores ramifications of life in a two-dimensional world, and what happens when a three-dimensional being intrudes. Amusing reading, but also useful as introduction to thought about hyperspace. Introduction by Banesh Hoffmann. 16 illustrations. xx + 103pp.   20001-9 Paperbound $1.00

POEMS OF ANNE BRADSTREET, edited with an introduction by Robert Hutchinson. A new selection of poems by America's first poet and perhaps the first significant woman poet in the English language. 48 poems display her development in works of considerable variety—love poems, domestic poems, religious meditations, formal elegies, "quaternions," etc. Notes, bibliography. viii + 222pp.

22160-1 Paperbound $2.00

THREE GOTHIC NOVELS: THE CASTLE OF OTRANTO BY HORACE WALPOLE; VATHEK BY WILLIAM BECKFORD; THE VAMPYRE BY JOHN POLIDORI, WITH FRAGMENT OF A NOVEL BY LORD BYRON, edited by E. F. Bleiler. The first Gothic novel, by Walpole; the finest Oriental tale in English, by Beckford; powerful Romantic supernatural story in versions by Polidori and Byron. All extremely important in history of literature; all still exciting, packed with supernatural thrills, ghosts, haunted castles, magic, etc. xl + 291pp.

21232-7 Paperbound $2.50

THE BEST TALES OF HOFFMANN, E. T. A. Hoffmann. 10 of Hoffmann's most important stories, in modern re-editings of standard translations: Nutcracker and the King of Mice, Signor Formica, Automata, The Sandman, Rath Krespel, The Golden Flowerpot, Master Martin the Cooper, The Mines of Falun, The King's Betrothed, A New Year's Eve Adventure. 7 illustrations by Hoffmann. Edited by E. F. Bleiler. xxxix + 419pp. 21793-0 Paperbound $3.00

GHOST AND HORROR STORIES OF AMBROSE BIERCE, Ambrose Bierce. 23 strikingly modern stories of the horrors latent in the human mind: The Eyes of the Panther, The Damned Thing, An Occurrence at Owl Creek Bridge, An Inhabitant of Carcosa, etc., plus the dream-essay, Visions of the Night. Edited by E. F. Bleiler. xxii + 199pp. 20767-6 Paperbound $1.50

BEST GHOST STORIES OF J. S. LEFANU, J. Sheridan LeFanu. Finest stories by Victorian master often considered greatest supernatural writer of all. Carmilla, Green Tea, The Haunted Baronet, The Familiar, and 12 others. Most never before available in the U. S. A. Edited by E. F. Bleiler. 8 illustrations from Victorian publications. xvii + 467pp. 20415-4 Paperbound $3.00

MATHEMATICAL FOUNDATIONS OF INFORMATION THEORY, A. I. Khinchin. Comprehensive introduction to work of Shannon, McMillan, Feinstein and Khinchin, placing these investigations on a rigorous mathematical basis. Covers entropy concept in probability theory, uniqueness theorem, Shannon's inequality, ergodic sources, the E property, martingale concept, noise, Feinstein's fundamental lemma, Shanon's first and second theorems. Translated by R. A. Silverman and M. D. Friedman. iii + 120pp. 60434-9 Paperbound $1.75

SEVEN SCIENCE FICTION NOVELS, H. G. Wells. The standard collection of the great novels. Complete, unabridged. *First Men in the Moon, Island of Dr. Moreau, War of the Worlds, Food of the Gods, Invisible Man, Time Machine, In the Days of the Comet*. Not only science fiction fans, but every educated person owes it to himself to read these novels. 1015pp. 20264-X Clothbound $5.00

LAST AND FIRST MEN AND STAR MAKER, TWO SCIENCE FICTION NOVELS, Olaf Stapledon. Greatest future histories in science fiction. In the first, human intelligence is the "hero," through strange paths of evolution, interplanetary invasions, incredible technologies, near extinctions and reemergences. Star Maker describes the quest of a band of star rovers for intelligence itself, through time and space: weird inhuman civilizations, crustacean minds, symbiotic worlds, etc. Complete, unabridged. v + 438pp. 21962-3 Paperbound $2.50

THREE PROPHETIC NOVELS, H. G. WELLS. Stages of a consistently planned future for mankind. *When the Sleeper Wakes,* and *A Story of the Days to Come,* anticipate *Brave New World* and *1984,* in the 21st Century; *The Time Machine,* only complete version in print, shows farther future and the end of mankind. All show Wells's greatest gifts as storyteller and novelist. Edited by E. F. Bleiler. x + 335pp. (USO) 20605-X Paperbound $2.50

THE DEVIL'S DICTIONARY, Ambrose Bierce. America's own Oscar Wilde— Ambrose Bierce—offers his barbed iconoclastic wisdom in over 1,000 definitions hailed by H. L. Mencken as "some of the most gorgeous witticisms in the English language." 145pp. 20487-1 Paperbound $1.25

MAX AND MORITZ, Wilhelm Busch. Great children's classic, father of comic strip, of two bad boys, Max and Moritz. Also Ker and Plunk (Plisch und Plumm), Cat and Mouse, Deceitful Henry, Ice-Peter, The Boy and the Pipe, and five other pieces. Original German, with English translation. Edited by H. Arthur Klein; translations by various hands and H. Arthur Klein. vi + 216pp.
20181-3 Paperbound $2.00

PIGS IS PIGS AND OTHER FAVORITES, Ellis Parker Butler. The title story is one of the best humor short stories, as Mike Flannery obfuscates biology and English. Also included, That Pup of Murchison's, The Great American Pie Company, and Perkins of Portland. 14 illustrations. v + 109pp. 21532-6 Paperbound $1.25

THE PETERKIN PAPERS, Lucretia P. Hale. It takes genius to be as stupidly mad as the Peterkins, as they decide to become wise, celebrate the "Fourth," keep a cow, and otherwise strain the resources of the Lady from Philadelphia. Basic book of American humor. 153 illustrations. 219pp. 20794-3 Paperbound $1.50

PERRAULT'S FAIRY TALES, translated by A. E. Johnson and S. R. Littlewood, with 34 full-page illustrations by Gustave Doré. All the original Perrault stories— Cinderella, Sleeping Beauty, Bluebeard, Little Red Riding Hood, Puss in Boots, Tom Thumb, etc.—with their witty verse morals and the magnificent illustrations of Doré. One of the five or six great books of European fairy tales. viii + 117pp. 8⅛ x 11. 22311-6 Paperbound $2.00

OLD HUNGARIAN FAIRY TALES, Baroness Orczy. Favorites translated and adapted by author of the *Scarlet Pimpernel.* Eight fairy tales include "The Suitors of Princess Fire-Fly," "The Twin Hunchbacks," "Mr. Cuttlefish's Love Story," and "The Enchanted Cat." This little volume of magic and adventure will captivate children as it has for generations. 90 drawings by Montagu Barstow. 96pp.
(USO) 22293-4 Paperbound $1.95

THE RED FAIRY BOOK, Andrew Lang. Lang's color fairy books have long been children's favorites. This volume includes Rapunzel, Jack and the Bean-stalk and 35 other stories, familiar and unfamiliar. 4 plates, 93 illustrations x + 367pp.

21673-X Paperbound $2.50

THE BLUE FAIRY BOOK, Andrew Lang. Lang's tales come from all countries and all times. Here are 37 tales from Grimm, the Arabian Nights, Greek Mythology, and other fascinating sources. 8 plates, 130 illustrations. xi + 390pp.

21437-0 Paperbound $2.50

HOUSEHOLD STORIES BY THE BROTHERS GRIMM. Classic English-language edition of the well-known tales — Rumpelstiltskin, Snow White, Hansel and Gretel, The Twelve Brothers, Faithful John, Rapunzel, Tom Thumb (52 stories in all). Translated into simple, straightforward English by Lucy Crane. Ornamented with headpieces, vignettes, elaborate decorative initials and a dozen full-page illustrations by Walter Crane. x + 269pp. 21080-4 Paperbound $2.50

THE MERRY ADVENTURES OF ROBIN HOOD, Howard Pyle. The finest modern versions of the traditional ballads and tales about the great English outlaw. Howard Pyle's complete prose version, with every word, every illustration of the first edition. Do not confuse this facsimile of the original (1883) with modern editions that change text or illustrations. 23 plates plus many page decorations. xxii + 296pp.

22043-5 Paperbound $2.50

THE STORY OF KING ARTHUR AND HIS KNIGHTS, Howard Pyle. The finest children's version of the life of King Arthur; brilliantly retold by Pyle, with 48 of his most imaginative illustrations. xviii + 313pp. 6⅛ x 9¼.

21445-1 Paperbound $2.50

THE WONDERFUL WIZARD OF OZ, L. Frank Baum. America's finest children's book in facsimile of first edition with all Denslow illustrations in full color. The edition a child should have. Introduction by Martin Gardner. 23 color plates, scores of drawings. iv + 267pp. 20691-2 Paperbound $2.50

THE MARVELOUS LAND OF OZ, L. Frank Baum. The second Oz book, every bit as imaginative as the Wizard. The hero is a boy named Tip, but the Scarecrow and the Tin Woodman are back, as is the Oz magic. 16 color plates, 120 drawings by John R. Neill. 287pp. 20692-0 Paperbound $2.50

THE MAGICAL MONARCH OF MO, L. Frank Baum. Remarkable adventures in a land even stranger than Oz. The best of Baum's books not in the Oz series. 15 color plates and dozens of drawings by Frank Verbeck. xviii + 237pp.

21892-9 Paperbound $2.25

THE BAD CHILD'S BOOK OF BEASTS, MORE BEASTS FOR WORSE CHILDREN, A MORAL ALPHABET, Hilaire Belloc. Three complete humor classics in one volume. Be kind to the frog, and do not call him names . . . and 28 other whimsical animals. Familiar favorites and some not so well known. Illustrated by Basil Blackwell. 156pp. (USO) 20749-8 Paperbound $1.50

EAST O' THE SUN AND WEST O' THE MOON, George W. Dasent. Considered the best of all translations of these Norwegian folk tales, this collection has been enjoyed by generations of children (and folklorists too). Includes True and Untrue, Why the Sea is Salt, East O' the Sun and West O' the Moon, Why the Bear is Stumpy-Tailed, Boots and the Troll, The Cock and the Hen, Rich Peter the Pedlar, and 52 more. The only edition with all 59 tales. 77 illustrations by Erik Werenskiold and Theodor Kittelsen. xv + 418pp. 22521-6 Paperbound $3.50

GOOPS AND HOW TO BE THEM, Gelett Burgess. Classic of tongue-in-cheek humor, masquerading as etiquette book. 87 verses, twice as many cartoons, show mischievous Goops as they demonstrate to children virtues of table manners, neatness, courtesy, etc. Favorite for generations. viii + 88pp. $6\frac{1}{2}$ x $9\frac{1}{4}$.
22233-0 Paperbound $1.25

ALICE'S ADVENTURES UNDER GROUND, Lewis Carroll. The first version, quite different from the final *Alice in Wonderland,* printed out by Carroll himself with his own illustrations. Complete facsimile of the "million dollar" manuscript Carroll gave to Alice Liddell in 1864. Introduction by Martin Gardner. viii + 96pp. Title and dedication pages in color. 21482-6 Paperbound $1.25

THE BROWNIES, THEIR BOOK, Palmer Cox. Small as mice, cunning as foxes, exuberant and full of mischief, the Brownies go to the zoo, toy shop, seashore, circus, etc., in 24 verse adventures and 266 illustrations. Long a favorite, since their first appearance in St. Nicholas Magazine. xi + 144pp. $6\frac{5}{8}$ x $9\frac{1}{4}$.
21265-3 Paperbound $1.75

SONGS OF CHILDHOOD, Walter De La Mare. Published (under the pseudonym Walter Ramal) when De La Mare was only 29, this charming collection has long been a favorite children's book. A facsimile of the first edition in paper, the 47 poems capture the simplicity of the nursery rhyme and the ballad, including such lyrics as I Met Eve, Tartary, The Silver Penny. vii + 106pp. 21972-0 Paperbound $1.25

THE COMPLETE NONSENSE OF EDWARD LEAR, Edward Lear. The finest 19th-century humorist-cartoonist in full: all nonsense limericks, zany alphabets, Owl and Pussycat, songs, nonsense botany, and more than 500 illustrations by Lear himself. Edited by Holbrook Jackson. xxix + 287pp. (USO) 20167-8 Paperbound $2.00

BILLY WHISKERS: THE AUTOBIOGRAPHY OF A GOAT, Frances Trego Montgomery. A favorite of children since the early 20th century, here are the escapades of that rambunctious, irresistible and mischievous goat—Billy Whiskers. Much in the spirit of *Peck's Bad Boy,* this is a book that children never tire of reading or hearing. All the original familiar illustrations by W. H. Fry are included: 6 color plates, 18 black and white drawings. 159pp. 22345-0 Paperbound $2.00

MOTHER GOOSE MELODIES. Faithful republication of the fabulously rare Munroe and Francis "copyright 1833" Boston edition—the most important Mother Goose collection, usually referred to as the "original." Familiar rhymes plus many rare ones, with wonderful old woodcut illustrations. Edited by E. F. Bleiler. 128pp. $4\frac{1}{2}$ x $6\frac{3}{8}$. 22577-1 Paperbound $1.25

Two Little Savages; Being the Adventures of Two Boys Who Lived as Indians and What They Learned, Ernest Thompson Seton. Great classic of nature and boyhood provides a vast range of woodlore in most palatable form, a genuinely entertaining story. Two farm boys build a teepee in woods and live in it for a month, working out Indian solutions to living problems, star lore, birds and animals, plants, etc. 293 illustrations. vii + 286pp.

20985-7 Paperbound $2.50

Peter Piper's Practical Principles of Plain & Perfect Pronunciation. Alliterative jingles and tongue-twisters of surprising charm, that made their first appearance in America about 1830. Republished in full with the spirited woodcut illustrations from this earliest American edition. 32pp. 4½ x 6⅜.

22560-7 Paperbound $1.00

Science Experiments and Amusements for Children, Charles Vivian. 73 easy experiments, requiring only materials found at home or easily available, such as candles, coins, steel wool, etc.; illustrate basic phenomena like vacuum, simple chemical reaction, etc. All safe. Modern, well-planned. Formerly *Science Games for Children*. 102 photos, numerous drawings. 96pp. 6⅛ x 9¼.

21856-2 Paperbound $1.25

An Introduction to Chess Moves and Tactics Simply Explained, Leonard Barden. Informal intermediate introduction, quite strong in explaining reasons for moves. Covers basic material, tactics, important openings, traps, positional play in middle game, end game. Attempts to isolate patterns and recurrent configurations. Formerly *Chess*. 58 figures. 102pp. (USO) 21210-6 Paperbound $1.25

Lasker's Manual of Chess, Dr. Emanuel Lasker. Lasker was not only one of the five great World Champions, he was also one of the ablest expositors, theorists, and analysts. In many ways, his Manual, permeated with his philosophy of battle, filled with keen insights, is one of the greatest works ever written on chess. Filled with analyzed games by the great players. A single-volume library that will profit almost any chess player, beginner or master. 308 diagrams. xli x 349pp.

20640-8 Paperbound $2.75

The Master Book of Mathematical Recreations, Fred Schuh. In opinion of many the finest work ever prepared on mathematical puzzles, stunts, recreations; exhaustively thorough explanations of mathematics involved, analysis of effects, citation of puzzles and games. Mathematics involved is elementary. Translated by F. Göbel. 194 figures. xxiv + 430pp. 22134-2 Paperbound $3.00

Mathematics, Magic and Mystery, Martin Gardner. Puzzle editor for Scientific American explains mathematics behind various mystifying tricks: card tricks, stage "mind reading," coin and match tricks, counting out games, geometric dissections, etc. Probability sets, theory of numbers clearly explained. Also provides more than 400 tricks, guaranteed to work, that you can do. 135 illustrations. xii + 176pp.

20338-2 Paperbound $1.50

MATHEMATICAL PUZZLES FOR BEGINNERS AND ENTHUSIASTS, Geoffrey Mott-Smith. 189 puzzles from easy to difficult—involving arithmetic, logic, algebra, properties of digits, probability, etc.—for enjoyment and mental stimulus. Explanation of mathematical principles behind the puzzles. 135 illustrations. viii + 248pp.
20198-8 Paperbound $1.75

PAPER FOLDING FOR BEGINNERS, William D. Murray and Francis J. Rigney. Easiest book on the market, clearest instructions on making interesting, beautiful origami Sail boats, cups, roosters, frogs that move legs, bonbon boxes, standing birds, etc. 40 projects; more than 275 diagrams and photographs. 94pp.
20713-7 Paperbound $1.00

TRICKS AND GAMES ON THE POOL TABLE, Fred Herrmann. 79 tricks and games— some solitaires, some for two or more players, some competitive games—to entertain you between formal games. Mystifying shots and throws, unusual caroms, tricks involving such props as cork, coins, a hat, etc. Formerly *Fun on the Pool Table*. 77 figures. 95pp.
21814-7 Paperbound $1.00

HAND SHADOWS TO BE THROWN UPON THE WALL: A SERIES OF NOVEL AND AMUSING FIGURES FORMED BY THE HAND, Henry Bursill. Delightful picturebook from great-grandfather's day shows how to make 18 different hand shadows: a bird that flies, duck that quacks, dog that wags his tail, camel, goose, deer, boy, turtle, etc. Only book of its sort. vi + 33pp. 6½ x 9¼. 21779-5 Paperbound $1.00

WHITTLING AND WOODCARVING, E. J. Tangerman. 18th printing of best book on market. "If you can cut a potato you can carve" toys and puzzles, chains, chessmen, caricatures, masks, frames, woodcut blocks, surface patterns, much more. Information on tools, woods, techniques. Also goes into serious wood sculpture from Middle Ages to present, East and West. 464 photos, figures. x + 293pp.
20965-2 Paperbound $2.00

HISTORY OF PHILOSOPHY, Julián Marias. Possibly the clearest, most easily followed, best planned, most useful one-volume history of philosophy on the market; neither skimpy nor overfull. Full details on system of every major philosopher and dozens of less important thinkers from pre-Socratics up to Existentialism and later. Strong on many European figures usually omitted. Has gone through dozens of editions in Europe. 1966 edition, translated by Stanley Appelbaum and Clarence Strowbridge. xviii + 505pp. 21739-6 Paperbound $3.00

YOGA: A SCIENTIFIC EVALUATION, Kovoor T. Behanan. Scientific but non-technical study of physiological results of yoga exercises; done under auspices of Yale U. Relations to Indian thought, to psychoanalysis, etc. 16 photos. xxiii + 270pp.
20505-3 Paperbound $2.50

Prices subject to change without notice.
Available at your book dealer or write for free catalogue to Dept. GI, Dover Publications, Inc., 180 Varick St., N. Y., N. Y. 10014. Dover publishes more than 150 books each year on science, elementary and advanced mathematics, biology, music, art, literary history, social sciences and other areas.